Winds of Change

Women Challenge Church

Joan Chittister, OSB

Sheed & Ward

Sheed & Ward™ is a service of National Catholic Reporter Publishing, Inc.

Library of Congress Catalog Card Number: 86-62124

ISBN: 0-934134-92-8

Published by: Sheed & Ward
115 E. Armour Blvd. P.O. Box 414292
Kansas City, MO 64141-4292

To order, call: (800)821-7926

Contents

1. TODAY I SAW THE GOSPEL: REFLECTIONS ON A THIRD WORLD EXPERIENCE

Cuernavaca Center for Intercultural Dialog on Development

Saturday, June 30

It's the end of a long day. We're all sitting on the veranda at the CCIDD Center in the middle of Cuernavaca. Ray Plankey and the staff will do the opening orientation soon.

The Council and I left Cleveland at six o'clock this morning. The trip was basically uneventful, but you could feel the apprehension in us. Though no one knows what to expect here, our instincts tell us that it's right to do this. Only the why and the how are unclear. If we learn nothing except the fact that people do things differently than gringos do and still survive well, that will be enough. It took two hours to get our luggage at the airport and the world did not end. Hurrah! Efficiency is not an ultimate value.

"We've been socially conditioned by the society in which we live," Ray Plankey says. "We have to learn to see the world differently; to learn to interpret the signs of the times." Well, this may be the beginning of a new world view for one whole Benedictine Federation if leadership has any meaning at all. There are seventeen Benedictine Sisters here: the whole Federation Council and our Priory Council and two or three additional community representatives.

The orientation do's and dont's are themselves an education:

1

- Don't waste the water. We only have so many gallons per day.

- Don't put any paper in the toilets. Put it in the wastebasket next to it to be disposed of in the garbage.

- Don't walk barefoot. You'll get worms.

- Don't let the shower run. Wet and soap and rinse in separate steps. This is the third world.

- Drink beer. With the present inflation rate it costs $.20 a bottle.

- Call collect. Mexico charges a 48 percent telephone tax! We pay a 3 percent surcharge in the U.S.

- Don't carry money. People are poor!
The list goes on and on. And the sign on the wall says: "Yes, there is a link between meaningless lives on one continent and meaningless deaths on the other."

Sunday, July 1

Today I saw the Gospel. It's been one of those full, deep days that suspend time and focus all thought.

We started our prayer and reflection on the readings of the day here on the veranda which opens on the yard. We were all a bit tentative, a bit disoriented yet. The night had been damp; there was no hot water and this morning the shower broke in our other room. But even that had sharpened our insights a bit. The readings were about Elisha and the Shunammite woman —two foreigners who gave one another life; Paul on the living and dying with Christ through Baptism — and having to let things die in order to let new and real life rise in us; Jesus saying "I have not come to bring peace" and "Those who accept the prophets receive the prophets' reward" — the need to be open to the word of God.

And then we went to the Plan de Ayalo parish and it all happened before our very eyes. In a bamboo hut with a dirt floor crowded with the poor, these people and their priest talked through the Scriptures and sang freedom songs. The holy picture on the front of the liturgical bulletin was Uncle Sam as a wolf in sheep's clothing talking peace but getting ready to devour Nicaragua. But to us they were kind and grateful we'd come.

They were dirty and poor and unsightful and free but not bitter. I cried through the Mass. It's all so senseless. My neat, clean, righteous country is behind it all while Americans think of themselves as messianic protectors of the incompetent world.

On the way back we stopped at Marymount Academy. It was an Alice-in-Wonderland type of morning. We went from a gathering of the poorest of the poor who remembered that Jesus had been called crazy because he knew that justice would bring division between those who would and those who would not be willing to lose their lost lives for something better, to a replica of the Hearst Mansion and a Moorish castle that had been built by a Texas Colonel and was now the plushest school in Cuernavaca. It was an incredible contrast of murals and marble with mud and human messiness.

Where was the "option for the poor" here? What position on behalf of degredation was this place taking; and what position do we take that's worth anything? A little soup kitchen; a small food pantry; a food bank; an academy that caters to the wounded and the marginalized but which can hardly make it financially; some minority day care centers; the corporate commitment. But does it all change anything? Moreover, isn't the way we ourselves live a countersign to what we do? We update this and replace that and redecorate this and redo that. We want more and more instead of less and less, and less and less. We haven't even begun to die so how can we expect to rise again. This will take such courage. I wonder if we really have it. No, I wonder if *I* really have it.

The Church here is "to the right of the government." Except in places like Plan de Ayalo, where the Christ of the Scriptures is alive and saying the same kind of crazy things He did in Israel: "Woe to the rich." Yet I am rich.

Monday, July 2

"What are you feeling at this time?" the directors asked us about yesterday's excursion to the squatter's settlement at La Estacion. Good God. Who knows the words? Amazement. Frustration. Disbelief. Pain. Inauthenticity. Isn't that enough?

La Estacion is several thousand people living in less than one square mile. In tin huts on mud floors. We were guests in Angela's home. She was 49. She'd had 12 children and is raising three grandchildren as well.

She lives on $10.00 a week. There are two rooms and four beds in the "house." She works from 5:00 a.m. one day until 2:00 a.m. the next because she has to wait until after 11:00 p.m. to get her water buckets filled for the next day. Thirteen persons live here.

Miriam asked: "What can we do for you?" Angela replied: "You do so much for me. You let me talk and that gives me relief. I learn from you. I learn words. I learn to speak."

She went on for five minutes. We all cried — openly, deeply.

But the facts remain: these people are living a sub-human existence while other human beings look on. They have eight outdoor spigots of running water for the entire settlement. They have outhouses built over a trickle of a creek. Their "houses" lean against one another with paths as streets between them. Their lean-to shelters are on railroad property and subject to destruction at anytime. Most have no electricity. For those who do, it's one sixty watt bulb.

The depression in our own group was palpable. I was indeed amazed, frustrated, disbelieving, full of pain. Amazed at the cleanliness and quiet of the place. Frustrated by my own sense of powerlessness in the face of so much evil. Incredulous that the rulers of the world allow/overlook/cause so much misery. Full of pain for this one simple woman who had taken us into her life without bitterness.

And that's what I understood least. Were the smiles of these people a sign of the Christian joy that comes from inner riches and transcends evil or were they symptoms of ignorant passivity, of people who've been hoodwinked into thinking that their lives are normal or at least acceptable. In the U.S. there's a recent history of dancing, childlike Blacks and docile, retiring women who bore pain as their God-given lot in life, and then got angry. Well, these people show no anger, and I honestly don't know if that's holy or not. This is a time for the Jesus who got angry, I think.

Tuesday, July 3

This morning Bishop Sergio Mendez-Arceo is to sit and talk with the group. Catholicism in Mexico, Plankey says, is conservative, progressive, radical, or popular. Mendez-Arceo is the only radical Bishop. But a converted one. He began his episcopacy in the '60s as a rigid authoritarian intellectual, began to change with the liturgical renewal — "restored the temple" (the Cuernavaca Cathedral), and threw the statues of saints out of the Church, was touched by Ivan Illich and became Don Sergio. When both were called to Rome, he refused to answer questions that "weren't worthy of a representative of the Pope!"

But in conversation with Paul VI, he and the pope became very good friends. Cuernavaca then became a center of advanced Christian thinking.

I guess most of us know this process. I started out committed to the "Church" and found myself committed only to the Christ. Let those who think the two are the same, beware. The problem is to determine where the two merge and where they do not. The "safe" thing is to assume — as we've been taught — that there is no difference. The way of the Spirit is to struggle between the two.

It was a great and disturbing morning. Mendez-Arceo was himself an event, a disturbing event. He says, among other things, "I am not a Marxist or a Communist, but I am not anti-Marxist or anti-Communist. I am anti-capitalist and anti-imperialist because they are anti-Christian, whereas communism and socialism would have to be deformed to be anti-Christian. Or, to put it another way: Capitalist goals are by nature anti-Christian; communist-socialist social goals are not. Marx may have been atheist, but his sociological analysis is not atheist. They do not presume the political structures of the Soviet Union, but we blind ourselves with 'anti-communism' and make it a fanaticism." It was a very sobering thought.

In any other Central American country the bishop would be assassinated. Here, he can simply be ignored, because the institutional church at large is quiet about the powerful, the rich, the political. That's how they maintain their own privileges, perhaps.

But the poor love this man. Everywhere we go, we hear his name from them.

I guess his greatest lesson to me at this moment in life is that he expects and accepts the fact that churchmen do not practice the Gospel either but does not evaluate that. He simply points out over and over that there are many Catholics in all institutions but few Christians. I, on the other hand, expect far too much from the Church. I was raised to believe that the Church was perfect, that all bishops and priests were good. Now I know they can be part of the problem and it hurts me. From Don Sergio I learned to go on without expecting any more help from the Church than from any other group.

Well, anyway, we needed to be in the presence of that man before we went to the Ravine. I thought nothing could be worse than La Estacion, but I was wrong.

We started at the Woman's Blouse Cooperative. The work was beautiful. The women were even more beautiful. In one unfinished room they came together to cut blouse patterns for women to sew and embroider at home. They use the co-op to teach women to read, to get money, to realize their dignity as women, to achieve some degree of independence. However, none can come without the permission of their husbands; many are beaten for it. But they persist. It was an experience of the rising spirit of women. It felt good. I saw it as a clear sign of present change and achievement.

Then we went to Marta's house in the Ravine. I've never seen anything like it in my life. We walked deep into the Ravine along an open drain of running sewage. We walked and climbed and jumped and clung to rocks and trees that lined the way to Marta's one-room hut, perched on a small slab of rock. She and six children have one bed, a propane stove, and her sewing machine there. The smells; the isolation; the blank, under-nourished faces; the tin, one-room lean-to's; the children and their distended stomachs; the hot, dark rooms; and the young women hung heavy with children, all soaked right into my mind and my body and my soul. Worse, I noticed that this dirty, dirty place was full of women. Women. There were few men, because most of these families are "las casas chicas," second families.

Marta, our "hostess," was a hollow woman. Thirty years old, with seven children, alone, uneducated, despairing, she makes blouses to pay for last week's food. Lorenzo, "her man," visits her drunk when it suits him. Water is in the faucets two hours a day; the people stand in line for hours waiting for it. The children have parasites.

Chris asked her: "Marta, what has been the happiest event in your life?" And she had no answer! She had no answer. She thought for a while and then said, "Maybe when it ends." In this place death is clearly preferable to life.

Wednesday, July 4

Today is Independence Day for a country that now has half

the world in a state of economic dependence. Mendez-Arceo called it "Neo-Colonialism," control by business and life-style and political influence rather than by military presence.

The labor leaders we heard today described it all. In Mexico, 96 percent of all industrial investment is foreign; 80 percent of that is American (U.S.A.). It's basically grist-mill industry. The Mexicans make parts, not products, so they get no corner on anything. Moreover, though Americans have brought in their factories, they have not brought in their wage standards, their benefits, their labor laws. Exploitation is a way of life for the few who can get work.

It's hard to be an American. But over and over again we hear from everyone, "You are a sign of hope to us. Now you will understand and help us. You will tell the American people and things will change."

But how? How will we do it? Now I think I'm really beginning to understand the prophets. They got a message, came to a consciousness that they were powerless to communicate. "I'm young; I stutter; no one will listen; Why me?" Yes to all of the above.

When we first came to Cuernavaca, we thought we were in a deprived living situation. Now, I'm embarrassed to be here, too. We prayed "to be delivered from the remorse that paralyzes"; but God, we need remorse. The problem is not simply remorse. The problem is remorse and fear and personal weakness. And I am so weak.

Thursday, July 5

We've spent the whole day at the Center itself — a good change of pace. S. Dolores Diaz de Sallano (a descendant of Spanish nobility, St. Philip of Jesus and Thomas Aquinas) who now lives and works in the Ravine, talked about Christian education and social action.

Her life and work are inspiring, but most troubling of all was her final comment: "In the United States, you can do something for us because you are at the heart of the empire." The empire. We are the new empire — like Rome, like Spain, like England. We live off the labor of the rest of the world. We rape and plunder — and smile and smile.

The horror is that it has corrupted religious life, too. We are highly individualistic, highly capitalistic. We want more money, more opportunities, more leisure. We have the fruits of capitalism; others have its burdens. Maybe we're too far gone to be converted. If so, this kind of religious life should die.

The guerilla priest, Enrique Morfin, says a bishop's authority is valid only when it benefits the poor. Now there's a thought.

And then he wiped out over three centuries of private spirituality with one insight: "Christians adore the bread instead of distributing the bread, like the manna, like Elijah, like Christ. There is no passage in the bible where people worship the bread, but we spend our lives 'adoring' the Blessed Sacrament while millions die of hunger each year."

Of every astounding thing that's going on this week, one of the most exciting is that despite the language barrier, despite all the translation, the real personalities of these simple people is coming through loud and clear. It's like a Pentecost experience. Somehow we can hear in our own tongue the spirit, the beauty, the pain, the personality of each of these strong and simple people.

Saturday, July 7

Yesterday we were here at the Center all day. In the morning Ray presented an overview of social and historical change in the church. In the afternoon, Kathleen did a few things on liberation theology. The material was good, clean. The discussion that emerged from them was highly charged. One of her questions was whether or not "revolution and/or violence are justified by institutional violence."

Ray obviously thinks they are. And, obviously, that's a common element in liberation theology. But I can't buy that. How is that any different from what's going on in the States? We only arm for righteousness and salvation. Who decides who's right? And who decides what's fair and how to assure it? What rules for war have ever worked? And if it's all so necessary, so Christian, this violence, why hasn't it ever been done for and by women. I'm sure there are more beaten, murdered wives than there are all the political prisoners of the world.

Anyway, Ray has a hard time understanding us, I think. And we have a hard time understanding, too. It isn't that we're virtuous. It's just that we haven't lived in the situation. I don't condemn these people for armed revolution. I just can't see that it's solved anything, any of their bloody revolutions. And I can't see that the world will survive unless Jesus becomes the norm.

Monday, July 9

And then Tlamacazapa. This Indian Village of 12,000-18,0000 is in the municipality of Taxco. Four miles away, on the other side of the mountain. And in that space of four miles the world spins apart.

It took one hour for the van to go the twelve miles up the mountain road to the village square. The mountain sides, sheer drop-offs, were all cultivated in corn. How it's planted or how it can possibly be harvested defies imagination. Other than the fields there is not a single sign of life. Then, suddenly you turn into a rocky plateau of thatch huts. All the posters come to life. Then, brown people — old before their years — stood back and watched us in silence. The large, old church was dark and empty. There were about 20 old pews; the rest was a cavern.

Only women came to the Mass. They were all wrapped in dark rebozos, shawls that women have to wear when they leave the house. I thought for a moment, looking out into the groups huddled against the walls, that I was in Egypt or Iran.

After Mass — and after they'd brought their small buckets of

water to be blessed — the priest, who walks two and a half hours
to get to this village, divided the congregation into four groups
so we could talk with them. It was a basically sterile conversation; they simply didn't know what to ask except about our climate. But we learned plenty. They do nothing — nothing — but
weave mats and baskets. They eat nothing — nothing — but
corn tortillas. Three times a day, every day of the week — and
only once or twice with frijoles and chiles. They grow nothing
else. The land is a rock pile with single corn stocks tucked between each stone, literally.

There is no fruit and no market. In other words, nothing else
is brought in. One woman said, "We have heard of lettuce but we
have never seen it. Anyway, we don't know how to eat it so it
doesn't make any difference."

They have never eaten a carrot. They cannot read. The men
"stay home and drink." The people have no water. The well is at
the top of the mountain, and it is often dry. No one washes. No
one bathes.

But the beer truck comes up, and the Coke truck comes up,
and the Fanta truck comes up the steep, steep mountain where
no one else chooses to go.

The "main street" of the pueblo was a path of rocks and boul-
ders that went straight up the mountain past the pigs and dogs
and burros and dirty, dirty people who carried water cans on
poles and heavy loads of firewood in sacks tied around their
heads.

The climb was excruciating. I tried to imagine day after day of
this. The well at the top of the mountain was crowded with men
and women scraping out a can of water at a time. The thatch
houses were smaller than our garages; there was no furniture
in them, no furniture at all. The floors were mud. The "food" was
warmed on a small fire of coals. Most of the village was women
and children, as the unemployed men regularly murder one
another in drunken brawls. Of the 94-year-old grandmother's
nine children, all seven sons are dead. She is waiting to die. In

this place, where life is isolated — the villagers, for instance, do not know where the United States is or anything about it — all the stereotypes crumble: We call these people dirty, when the fact is they have no water. We call them lazy, when the fact is there are no jobs. We call them stupid, when the fact is that their diets make full mental and physical development impossible.

The trip down the mountain was quiet and full of pain. We were all exhausted and emotionally drained. Where in heaven's name do you start to address something like this? With education, with roads, with money, with food? Everything these people owned in life, everything was in a plastic bag that hung on the side of the hut. All the work was basket-weaving. All the goals were survival. All the people were thin and tired.

It was a hard day.

But the next day was even harder. It was what Ray called later, "the crucifixion day of the program."

A catechist from Guatemala and missionaries from El Salvador sat for literally hours and poured out one example after another of terror, torture and destruction of people and places. And it's all financed by the American government that does not want the economic structures which bind these countries to U.S. companies to change.

People with bibles are murdered as insurrectionists. Villages are traumatized. Their "peasant leagues" that speak for wages and decent living conditions in the plantation systems are called "communist."

And catechists — who taught reading, writing and Scripture — became keys to the opposition and as community leaders had to be eliminated. Ignorance is the basis of oppression. Those who threaten ignorance are enemies of the state. So, the U.S., which wants this pool of resources and markets, sent advisors and weapons to keep the people down.

Around the table, one after another of the group began to cry as the words and analyses took form in the slide shows and news reels. We were simply saturated with the horror of it all and smothered by the amount of information and incidents. The group was tired and frustrated and angry and feeling oppressed by heaps of evil and lack of time. Everyone went to bed silent and sullen.

Wednesday, July 11, St. Benedict's Day

Yesterday was a day of lectures. And they were good. They put a framework around the facts. And the crucifixion day paled a bit. Despair turned to possibility. There are specific American concepts that can and must be confronted.

It's rained the better part of this day. Everything is cold and damp. I thought of the old grandmother and the suffering women in the Indian village at Tlamatozapa. Every hut must be muddy, every person wet. At least there will be water in the well.

Thursday, July 12

It's the last day of the seminar. The input level is still high but the group energy level is very low.

Someone in the group said yesterday at the biblical reflection period that her community was dying. And I thought to myself: We all are if we do not abandon business-as-usual and get on with these Gospel agendas.

As an American I have lost all heart. The world is our economic sandbox and we are prepared to do whatever we must to maintain it. All of Central America has been prostituted for our gains, and our people truly believe that we are good and godly and grand in our designs.

We're about to begin the wind-up session. I keep trying to imagine Jesus and the disciples or Mary and Mary Magdalene in a wind-up session with newsprint and crayons brainstorming strategies. So I wonder what's wrong with our kind. Maybe we're just too much organization people. Maybe we just each have to do what we each have to do and see if the heavens open.

But one thing I know: It is true that the poor must evangelize us. They show us how little it really takes to live; how little it really takes to be happy; how little it really takes to be somebody; how little it really takes to be valiant, to be holy, to be of God.

Monday, July 16, Mexico City

At 6:30 Juanita took us all out for Chris' Jubilee Dinner to "La Hacienda de Morales." Very, very high class by Mexican standards and therefore very, very uncomfortable for me after two weeks of CCIDD. There's the problem. Should no one ever have anything special? Should we never have anything special until everyone has enough? I'm not sure about that. And Jesus is no help. He went to the Wedding Feast at Cana; he said, "The poor you have always with you." He allowed Mary of Magdala to pour out the perfume. What in heavens name is the answer to that? I remember being at a catered banquet with Mother Teresa of Calcutta in 1975. I wonder if she worried that night?

On Sunday morning we went to the Basilica. It was a press of deprived humanity. Indians danced in the courtyard as I had remembered from two past feasts of Our Lady of Guadalupe that I'd spent in Mexico. They don't go into the Basilica. Why should they? That's the Mass of the conqueror. They come for the Lady who dignified the Indian. These are the people who believe that Jesus' claim to fame is that He is the son of Our Lady of Guadalupe. These are also the people who know that the official Church is not theirs.

They come by the thousands and cook tortillas in the piazza and climb up the hill to Tepeyac in the hope that the Lady will touch them too.

We're almost over Cleveland now. Home. And now what? I remember the conversation with the young Mexican Sister who told me she wasn't sure she could stay in her community because there "people forgot who they were" and "began to live above themselves" and said that "working with the poor was incompatible with their religious tradition." I told her that her call

was authentic, that it was basic to religious life, that not only
the poor but also our communities and the Church were in need
of evangelization. I asked her to stay for our sakes, for the poor
for whom a community could be a strong sign. I asked her in
other words to "risk her life in the hope that we are capable of
conversion." I hope that was not an irresponsible expenditure of
a life.

We're about to land in Cleveland. I remember the story:

It was a chilly, overcast day when the horseman spied
the little sparrow lying on its back in the middle of the
road. Reining in his mount he looked down and inquired
of the fragile creature, "Why are you lying upside down
like that?"

"I heard the heavens are going to fall today," replied the
bird. The horseman laughed. "And I suppose your spindly
legs can hold up the heavens." "One does what one can,"
said the little sparrow.

Well, I will try. God, keep me from righteous indignation at
people who take things and time and cars and money and opportunities and vacations and clothes and food for granted.

2. THE CHALLENGE OF PEACE

The Indian priest Modamayetz instructed his people: "Be not a whisper that is lost in the wind. Be a voice that is heard above the confusion of the storms of life." The pastoral letter of the American Catholic Bishops — *Peace: God's Call; Our Response* — is, I believe, the first clear voice of a major Church body that has been heard above the storm of militarism that now engulfs the United States.

In fact, in 1973, the sociologist D.C. Bock investigated the relationship of religious commitment to an individual's willingness to follow the commands of authority figures, even when that meant inflicting pain and and death on innocent victims. Bock concluded that high religious believers, churchgoing people, were consistently the most obedient of all. It was churchgoers who complied with authority most. It was churchgoers who administered more punishment than any other single group in the research population. And because they had been ordered to do so by an authority figure, they did so without question, without concern, without conscience, despite all moral imperatives to the contrary.

Later, in the 1983 ecumenical, interdisciplinary study of the nature of contemporary Christian belief conducted by the Ecumenical and Cultural Research Institute in Collegeville, Minnesota, almost half of the entire church-going population of the study said that the teachings of their church on war are unclear.

In an era when one false move can destroy the planet, the people obviously need to hear a clear voice from the church on issues of life and authority and nationalism and war.

But even if the need is real and the consequences ultimate, it is not an easy call to hear, because even in you, and certainly in me, two separate church voices now ring in our hearts. One of those voices comes from the Christmas message of Pius XII in 1956. The Pope said on that occasion: "If, therefore, a body representative of the people and the government, both having been chosen by free elections, in a moment of extreme danger decides by legitimate instrument of internal and external policy on defensive precautions and carries out the plans they consider necessary, it does not act immorally. Therefore, a Catholic citizen cannot invoke his own conscience in order to refuse to serve and fulfill the duties the law imposes."

The second voice, which comes from the National Conference of American Catholic bishops in the pastoral, *The Challenge of Peace,* speaks a new word at a new time to a new world situation and, therefore, is a new moment of church. Why has this change occurred? Because in addition to the present social context, the church is faced with biblical paradigms which speak in new and powerful tones. One scripture, in particular, I suggest, may explain the present peace pastoral best. It's from the Book of Judges, Chapter 7.

The Israelites, remember, were under siege by the Midianites. Times had been hard for seven years. The Chosen People were completely intimidated by the foreign army and had even taken to hiding in the mountains, which was bad enough. But, worse than that, every time the Israelites sowed seed, the Midianites returned with a massive army, "thick as locusts," to destroy the produce. Scripture says they left nothing for Israel to live on: not a sheep, not an ox, not a donkey.

It was terrorism of the worst kind. It was a mortal enemy with whom the people dealt. The whole nation was in danger of extinction.

And the people cried out to Yahweh. And Yahweh heard them.

But what Yahweh identified as the instrument of their salvation was a young, frightened, even cynical young man whose faith in Yahweh had been sorely tried and was basically eroded. In fact, when the Angel of Yahweh said, "Yahweh is with you, valiant warrior," Scripture records that Gideon answered: "Excuse me, my Lord, but if Yahweh is with us, why is all this happening to us? And where are all his miracles which our ancestors used to tell us about?"

But with one alternative little better than the other, Gideon finally agreed to take upon himself the protection of the people and summoned an army. From all the lands around they came. Heavy with battle array they came. Thirty-two thousand of them came. And all of them were waiting for the sound of the horn that would pit them in all-out battle with the enemy. And Gideon's faith was restored.

And that's when it happened:

First, Yahweh insisted that Gideon release from the army anyone who was afraid. And twenty-two thousand soldiers returned to their homes. Gideon's faith wavered.

Then Yahweh declared that of the ten-thousand who remained only those who lapped water rather than cupped it could remain. And that left 300 men. Gideon's faith collapsed.

The army had been decimated. Gideon was left with little but his will to succeed, his trust in Yahweh and his fear. Yahweh's reasoning was simple. "If I allow you to go into battle with 32,000 men," Yahweh explains, "they will say, 'See what Gideon has done for God.' But if you go with 300 they will say, 'See what God has done for Gideon.' "

And with horns and torches in the middle of the night, Gideon's band routed the entire Midianite army.

In that way, with outrageous faith and unflagging commitment and non-violent action, Israel became strong and secure in the world again.

In their peace pastoral, *The Challenge of Peace,* the American bishops invite all of us, this entire nation, to lay down the weapons of total destruction. In the peace pastoral, the American bishops invite all of us, this entire nation, to have the faith of the vulnerable Gideon because now, like then, conscience demands another alternative.

The question is: How in the life time of people today did the church get from Pius XII to a peace pastoral of this magnitude? The answer is that the pastoral is demanded by the standard theological tradition of the Church. In the peace pastoral American Catholic bishops have not shifted to the left. The fact is that the military technical establishment of this society has tilted toward total planetary destruction, and that is a sin against creation that the church simply cannot ignore.

It is not true that the peace pastoral deviates from the established tradition of the church. On the contrary. The church has always argued that there is such a thing as a just war. The difference is that this pastoral not only reiterates but carefully scrutinizes the just war theory and finds it lacking in a nuclear world.

The principles of the just war theory are clear. For any war to be considered morally right, the tradition says, there are clear givens: The cause must be just. The war must have been called by the competent authority and with the intention of achieving peace and reconciliation, not destruction. It must be waged only as a last resort after all peaceful efforts have been exhausted. There must be clear probability of success. The damage must be in proportion to the good that can be achieved. And the war must be waged by just means. Following these aged standards, this pastoral scrutinizes American military policy according to the tenets of justice, rightness, good intentions, good effects, last resort, proportionality, discrimination. And they all pale in the face of the nuclear fuse.

What is just about the momentary destruction of a whole civilization — its elderly, its farmers, its hospitals, its musicians, its museums, its children, its water, its air, its trees?

What cause is so right that unlimited evil may be committed in the name of resistance to evil, that all other social values may be sacrificed for one?

How can the intention of a nuclear exchange possibly mean anything else but total destruction?

How can planetary suicide possibly be "the last resort" for the superficial questions of arbitrary boundaries, electoral systems, and political ideologies which come and go with history and whim?

What indeed is the probability of success in a nuclear war? The only possible argument is that the makers of this war were the winners of the last one and so rush like lemmings to the sea to relive the same kind of conquest. Unfortunately, this time that rush involves denying the differences in weapons and strategy and effects between VE day in 1945 and the nuclear doomsday that we face today. The rush includes saying "Better dead than Red," and making that decision for us all. The rush includes preferring a loss of civilization to a loss of face or a neurotic nationalism to international negotiation.

How can the good to be accomplished possibly be proportionate to the damage inflicted or the costs incurred by weapons that, according to the Turco, Toon, Ackerman, Pollack and Sagan study of "The Atmospheric Consequences of Nuclear War," — which has now been recognized even by the Pentagon — will poison the atmosphere; destroy all the water supplies of the world; burn away the ozone layer; eliminate transportation, communications and utilities; wipe out industry; turn the world into radiated darkness; drop the temperatures around the globe to below freezing for over a year; and, if we're lucky, expunge life, not only in enemy territory, but everywhere? And all of that with the detonation of less than one percent of the present arsenal, though every year we will build more and more and more weapons.

To those who say, "Don't you believe in the defense of this country?": to those who ask, in a world that may destroy itself thirty-five times over, "Don't you believe in the American way of life?," I say, "Isn't once enough? Will you feel more secure tonight knowing that tomorrow morning we'll be able to destroy the world yet another time?" The document calls this situation "a monstrously disproportionate response."

Yes, it is true that the pastoral letter repeats the just war theory, but it does not promise that now, today, in our time, or ever again, war as we have structured it can possibly be just. The question then is: Is this a pacifist document or a defense document?

The answer is that the document braids pacifism and the just war theory together. This document makes it as acceptable for some to choose not to fight at all as it does for others to critique the present defense situation and choose among its options. In other words, the pacifist tradition is recognized and legitimated in this document, and only some thinking about war as a way to reduce violence is given credence. The point is that those who argue the just war theory can only be authentic if they begin their thinking by arguing against force. For both traditions, the pacifist and the defensive, the presumption is always against force. Consequently, those who argue the just war theory in a nuclear world walk a narrow, shaking plank.

It is true that the just war theory has been held for centuries in the Roman Catholic Church. But it is also clear that it is usually held in footnotes; it has often been held in Latin; it has generally been held in the musings of moral theologians or church historians. It has seldom or never been held as the very stuff of conscience formation for politicians, for parishes, for draftees. But today, you and I can ignore the just war theory no longer. We may no longer leave it to the military, who will be only an infinitesimal part of the casualties. It is you and everything you hold dear that is at stake, that is under target even now. With this document the just war theory becomes a filter not just for history but for your actions and mine.

The pastoral calls for a new world order, an international authority to arbitrate among the peoples of the world rather than simply to acknowledge the coercion of the strong over the weak.

The document questions American defense policy and unmasks deterrence for what it really is. Deterrence is the planned, indiscriminate destruction of millions of innocent people to whom nuclear weapons, nuclear violence, nuclear power and nuclear strategy are all invisible and, consequently, impossible to imagine and more impossible to confront. In 1943 the people who feared war could see the soldiers marching and hear the tanks rumbling. They could watch the ground shake from the blast of cannon fire and feel the taste of fear that comes in the face of amassed, irrational power. But tonight Colorado sleeps without a sound next to an even quieter Rocky Flats. Washington, D.C. cradles the Pentagon in its midst and never sees a single sign of danger. Iowa and Kansas and Nebraska plant missile silos in their cornfields with confidence, if they're aware of them at all, because that invisible, insidious, ultimate deterrence only happens once.

The military policy of deterrence is the policy of omnicide. We all live in Guyana now. And like Jim Jones, our government wants a commitment to suicide as the sign of the "true believer." But this document says *no* to counter-population warfare and thus rejects our present targeting practices. It says *no* to first use and so denies our present weapons build-up.

This document also says *no* to the whole idea of "limited nuclear war." What, in heaven's name, is a "limited" nuclear war? Who will count for us? Who will control the battlefield when emotions are high and the pressures of time make bad judgments catastrophic, in a war that will be fought by strapping bombs the size of those that destroyed Hiroshima and Nagasaki on the backs of 19-year-old boys in the farm fields of Germany — on the backs of boys too young to buy a bottle of beer in twenty-one states of this country? The document says there is no justification for submitting the human community to this risk, not even the fear of communism, apparently. For communism is a political system, but the Russians are people.

This document says there must be no shift in deterrence policy. To drop nuclear bombs on those who are dropping bombs on you is one thing. That used to be the deterrence policy of our country. But to drop nuclear bombs on those who you think might drop a nuclear bomb on you, presently our "first strike" policy, is something else. We call it "destabilizing," meaning "nerve-wracking." There it is, the silly peacenik argument: "If we have nuclear weapons, they'll get used." To which the government and military answer: "Can't those peace people see? The whole point of deterrence is to see that they are never used. Why would anyone unleash the devastation of an entire country out of undocumented fear?"

Well, I don't know. Why do guard dogs bark at empty cars? Why do smoke alarms go off when the bacon burns? Why do soldiers shoot people who can't remember passwords? Why do fighter pilots destroy civilian airliners that they can't see in the dark? Why would anyone launch a nuclear weapon? Because in the first-strike world which you and I and this country have created, no one can be sure what will happen next if they don't.

When the attacks on Hiroshima and Nagasaki were ordered, we had over six hours to change our mind, to recall the planes, at least to warn everyone to take cover. But this time you and I may have as little as six minutes to leave the office, find the car in the parking lot, drive across town to pick up the family and pack the soda crackers on which we will live for the rest of our cold and dark and radiated lives. And it will all be controlled by a computer that can't bill you correctly for seven months in a row. Worse, these Cruise, these Pershing, these MX missiles are of American invention and design.

Finally, remember that the whole concept of deterrence is based on the rationality of the other side, despite the fact that

we argue repeatedly that the Russians are essentially, pro-
foundly, fundamentally irrational (which incidentally, was the
same argument we made about the Germans and the Japanese
forty years ago and who are our allies now). Deterrence works,
they say, because no one in their right minds would use it. Well,
we cannot have it both ways. Either the Russians are irrational
and deterrence is futile, or the Russians are rational and deterrence is unnecessary. The peace pastoral focuses a light on the
defenselessness of nuclear defense; on the madcap, miniscule,
make-shift morality of the present nuclear policy.

Finally, the document calls each of us to conscience: parents
as guides, media as fact-finders, schools as standard setters, di-
oceses as evangelists, the military as moral defenders of the nation, the young as bearers of its future, nuns and priests as creative teachers and preachers of this document. It calls each of us,
like Gideon, to reduce the size of our army, to put away our fear,
to trust.

In what it does, the document definitely begins the development of a new theology of peace and a new process of conscience
formation. But there are, at the same time, important things
that the document does not do. There are questions which the
document raises but does not answer. There are issues which
the document does not address, which fall to us, which cry to
conscience out of the very principles this document so well defines.

For instance, this document condemns first-strike weapons
but not first-strike complicity. The problem is that if a weapon
cannot morally be used, how can it morally be designed, developed, constructed and deployed? How can it possibly be moral
to make economic what may not be made military?

The pastoral promises continued critical evaluation of each
separate weapons system, and warns of eventual condemnation, but it gives no criteria: no specific size, no amount of time,
no particular type of weapon that will once and for all exhaust
the human conscience and lead to absolute condemnation.

The document obscures what could and should be a clear moral message with unclear language. It talks of "strictly conditioned moral acceptance" when it means "clearly defined moral rejection" of certain systems and policies — a subtlety that may well be lost on the assembly-line church-goers who make the nose-cones and neutrons of the nuclear industry. A state-wide study of church-goers found that 85 percent said that the teaching of their churches about war is unclear to them. In the face of language designed to be vague, it is no wonder.

The bishops call for individual responsibility in the document but do not call their own military chaplains to the same level of accountability for life to which they could, with ease apparently, call an Agnes Mary Mansour. Where abortion is concerned the message is clear: doctors may not perform them; nurses may not advise them; Catholic hospitals may not allow them, and Catholic money may not support them. But military chaplains are not told to denounce nuclear weapons publicly or to leave nuclear bases or even to evangelize and instruct in selective conscientious objection the young people on those bases on whose informed decisions, the pastoral says, the future fate of the world depends. Young people who sit at the bottom of cement silos and wait for word to push green Launch buttons. Young people who will never even see the eyes of their victims. Young people for whom no adult direction exists, but who themselves must make the decisions which will save or obliterate not one life but all life.

The document defines a theology of toleration about war and nuclear deterrence which is not universally applied to other complex issues. Birth control is always wrong; abortion is always wrong; the presence of women in seminaries is always wrong; but the morality of contributing to the designed destruction of the planet is apparently open to debate and discussion and moral doubt in my church. What is a woman to think? When life is in the hands of a woman, to destroy it is always morally wrong, never to be condoned, an always grave and universal evil. But when life is in the hands of men, millions of lives at one time — no, all of life at one time — then destruction can be theologized and rationalized. Then some people's needs and lives are made more important than other people's needs and lives. A peace church, a pro-life church must confront this dichotomy to be credible.

Finally, though the document itself speaks out of the feminine dimension of the human soul, it fails to decry the fact that it is precisely the present institutionalization of solely masculine values — power and profit and primacy — that make militarism inevitable. The document calls us to a better, fuller self but does not name it, and therein lies the error. Until we know what is missing in society, we cannot possibly maintain it.

Let there be no mistake. I am not talking about the aggrandizement of the female. I am talking about the encouragement, the recognition, the release of the feminine in all of us. We need now, in this society, in ways more urgent than ever before, the feminine values of collaboration rather than competition, of compassion rather than coercion, of commitment rather than control; or the soul and the spirit and the insights of humanity will shrink and shrivel to the size of the machines we have posed to destroy us. There will be no new world without a new view of the complementarity of the essential components of creation in the entire social system. "Yahweh made them in God's own image," Scripture teaches us. "Male and female God made them."

To be whole, to be lasting, to be real, to be effective, peacemakers cannot long ignore women, the women's movement and the feminine in creation. Nor can the church.

But whatever issues the pastoral raises, it resolves many as well. Most of all, perhaps, it shows the separation of church and state argument for the decoy argument it is. When bishops bless bombers and salute the flag and pay taxes, no one says the church shouldn't be involved in politics. The peace pastoral is a clear declaration that confronting obstacles to justice is no less religious than subsidizing the works of mercy.

Finally, the document brings us head-to-head with the God of Sodom and Gomorrah and so gives us marvelous hope in the face of massive evil. Remember that in the Sodom and Gomorrah story three things happen:

• God is appalled by a whole society that is steeped in grave and galling sin and determines to destroy it.

• In Sodom and Gomorrah it is not God but one human who argues the value of human life, who challenges a just God to do justice to the just.

• In Sodom and Gomorrah God agrees to a human formula to spare the whole sickly, sinful society for the sake of simply ten just.

And therein lies the problem. The tragedy of Sodom and Gomorrah is not that God destroyed them; they deserved to be destroyed. No, the tragedy of Sodom and Gomorrah is that only six of the necessary ten could be found: Lot and his wife, Lot's two daughters, and Lot's two sons-in-law. On the other hand, that is why the story is such a powerful message for our own time for those of us who think they can do nothing; for those of us who want to do something but feel totally helpless in the face of the inevitable disaster of a nuclear holocaust; for those of us who fear the triumph of massive evil over a meager few, who love life enough to bargain for it and who fear the ultimate nuclear sin against creation. In Sodom and Gomorrah, God negotiated! God was willing to forebear for the sake of simply ten.

Now assume that again, in our time, as antidote to our destructive deterrence, six peacemakers have already been identified. The question for today is not, will four more just be found at the Pentagon? Not, will four more just be found in Red Square? Not, can we find the other four at Rockwell International? The question for us is, will four more be found in my hometown tonight? Four people willing to be called traitor, communist, radical, even heretic; four among us willing to believe with Gideon; four people willing to practice the holy disobedience that this peace pastoral calls for may well rest all our hope.

3. A FEMININE CRITIQUE OF THE PEACE PASTORAL

Christianity is a pattern of powerless people in struggle with the powers of darkness: David faced Goliath with a sling shot; the Jews dealt with the Egyptians by marking their doorposts with the blood of a lamb; Joshua blew a sacred horn to raze the walls of Jericho; Jesus climbed the cross. But there is another strain in the tradition as well: Gideon gathered an army; Moses saved the Chosen People by raising up his arms to heaven while battle raged on the plains below; a pope called the crusades; nations warred for thirty years in the name of religious freedom; Christians killed for the Fuhrer and the fatherland, to make the world safe for democracy, for God and country, for faith and flag. It is Christians who have brought science to the high art of planetary cataclysm and Christians who used the final weapon first.

In the history of Christian conflict, then, is the microcosm of *anima* in struggle with *animus*. The attempts to integrate the two have been constant: there have been rules for war, agreements on the treatment of prisoners, peace treaties, and weapons negotiations. But the rules have been broken; the agreements have been flaunted; the treaties have been ignored and the negotiations blocked. Over and over and over again. Never has the best of both human dimensions, the masculine and the feminine, been brought to the center of world affairs. On the contrary, in a world designed solely by males whose theology has told them that to be male is to be a superior being, the feminine qualities of the human soul have often been both repressed and resisted as signs of weakness.

There is, in other words, both a masculine and a feminine, a confrontative and a cajoling skein in the Christian carder. The

29

feminine strain has always trusted in God; the masculine strain has often chosen for chariots.

The question is, where are we now as Church? The publication of the NCCB Pastoral on Peace and War may give us our clearest clue.

To analyze its underlying theology, it is essential to identify the propositions the document makes and to ask what kind of propositions those are: the kind that nurture and create or the kind that conquer and divide?

The tenets of the document are profound. In the first place, it proclaims pacifism as a legitimate and necessary charism in the Church; in the second, it declares the just war theory equally moral but a narrow corridor indeed upon which to rest the case for politically legitimate murder. To be "just," the document reminds us, a war can be fought only to maintain basic human rights for everyone concerned; only after negotiation and compromise; only with the probability of success; only if the damage inflicted is not disproportionate to the good that is accomplished; and only if combatants are discriminated from non-combatants, "so that those who do not make war do not have war made upon them." From that ground, the document draws conclusions about contemporary American military policy that are both logical and prophetic.

Commonly considered feminine and masculine traits have been identified and defined by psychologists for years now. In simple terms, it is *feminine* to value and reflect spontaneity, flexibility, submission, intuition, support, feeling, eros, and self-sacrifice. In this culture, on the other hand, it is considered *masculine,* to value or reflect a sense of order, control, aggressiveness, logic, competition, reason, logos, and self-development.

Either behavior pattern taken to its extreme is a sign of mental illness. Worse, either behavior pattern applied indiscriminately to the problem of human security is destructive on a grand scale. What is even more important, perhaps, is to realize that research is consistent in its report that masculine traits are in general more valued than feminine ones, even among women themselves. To choose to act out of feminine values in this society, then, would be at least charismatic, if not absurd. Even women work hard to prove that they have the personality qualities acceptable to the white, male society around them: not too soft, not too caring, not too trusting, not too giving; tough-minded, shrewd, on top of things.

But the foolish femininity of a Gospel centered on a cross is of the essence of the Christian dispensation. It is not of the essence of the political relations of the Christian world, however. In the document, *The Challenge of Peace,* American bishops are clearly struggling between the two.

In a world where competition, coercion, and control put collaboration, compassion, and consensus at a premium, the document makes steady strides toward the Jesus whose private life was humble and whose public life was powerless but empowering. The document looks at life through other than masculine eyes. It is important that the document be read the same way or both what is and is not being said may be lost. It seems to me that people who value the feminine dimensions of life and wish dearly that those kinds of values would inform the public as well as the domestic arena will sense a strong feminist perspective in the bishops' attempt to bring the Christian Gospel to the nuclear question. At significant moments, the choices between a masculine power paradigm and the feminine principle of peacemaking emerge in the document with prophetic clarity. The following overview is representative of the struggle but not exhaustive of the feminine values that the work emphasizes:

Spontaneity/Order; Intuition/Logic

In its present form, the document is an admittedly unfinished and, in fact, an initiating exploration of the present military posture and policies of the United States. Without claiming to have

all the answers, in other words, the Roman Catholic bishops of
the country have been moved as a body to the level of a pastoral
letter on peace because "the world is at a moment of supreme
crisis and the effect of this crisis is evident in the lives of people."
In fact, despite the claims of the Pentagon of the orderliness of
tactical weapons on the battlefield, the document disputes the
ability of field commanders to make rational and disciplined responses about the use by foot soldiers of NATO forces in Europe
of nuclear weapons — some of which are the size of the bomb
dropped on Hiroshima but now called "small" by the military
strategists of the nation.

Flexibility/Control

Rather than assert the traditional ideology of American civil
religion that it is a moral duty for the United States to convert
the world to capitalism or at least to resist communism, whatever the cost, the document says simply but with far-reaching
ramifications: "There is no justification for submitting the
human community to the risk of nuclear war," even though "limited," or even to the threat to use nuclear weapons. Clearly,
control through either force or fear is abrogated in the document.

Submissiveness/Aggression

By arguing against counter-population warfare, the legiti-
macy of threat as a national policy, and the use as well of re-
taliatory action that would take innocent lives, the pastoral
comes down squarely against the male code of making people
say "uncle," a not small step in the erosion of male power play.

Support/Competition

In contrast to the present competitive public policy, the pastoral argues for sufficiency of defenses rather than for nuclear

superiority. What it does not argue for is support of the Russian people as people, whatever the paranoia of their own government. The document says quite clearly that "sovereignty is not an absolute value" and calls for sincere support of the United Nations but does not go so far as to imply that the United States itself may have to be content with less so that others, having more by right, will seek less by force.

Feeling/Reason; Eros/Logos

Whatever the arguments for deterrence — that only the arms race keeps the world at peace, that only the willingness to use nuclear weapons prevents their use, that first strike arsenals are logical responses to conflict in a nuclear world — the bishops argue feelingly that the situation is "neither tolerable nor necessary." Furthermore, the pastoral takes the position for the first time in modern history that pacificism and "selective conscientious objection," the right of an individual to make a moral decision about their willingness to participate in this particular war or with this particular weapon, are acceptable responses in a world gone mad with the "logic" and "reason" of military supremacy.

Self-Sacrifice/Self-Development

By affirming the relevance of the age-old theory of the "just war," the document asserts the need for a country to negotiate and compromise before war, any kind of war, is waged. What the pastoral does not do is question the notion of unrestricted development itself or the need to sacrifice self for the sake of others even as a nation. Self-sacrifice, however, is not a natural part of the male model. Men overcome weakness; only women accept it.

There are some feminine values which the document stops short of claiming. For instance, the document does not call for unilateral disarmament, the really feminine ideal; the document does not call for World Government, the ultimate act of national equality and concern; the document does not expose the male value system as the basis of world tension and the very antithesis of the new forms of conflict resolution which it requires be developed. In significant ways, nevertheless, the pastoral is basically feminist. It rejects control, agressiveness, competition and reason as ultimate values of human growth and calls by implication for flexibility, submissiveness, support, feeling, eros and self-sacrifice. It is precisely on those grounds that it is being criticized as "foolish," "incompetent," "weak," and even "ridiculous." Women have known the criticism for eons.

At the same time, no document of the American Catholic Church sounds more like the Gospel unglossed, unwarped, and undistorted.

Strange. Interesting. Disturbing.

4. THE FUTURE CHURCH: A PEOPLE OF VISION AND MEMORY

The essayist Rosten writes: "The function of life is not to be happy; the function of life is to matter — to have it make a difference that you lived at all." If churches had a motto perhaps that should be it.

The problem is that in our time no one is quite sure what is really needed to make the difference: Should it be memory? Or should it be vision? Does making a difference in this day demand a return to the faith of a clearer past or does it demand decisive movement to a distinctly different future?

The Sufi masters tell a story that in this age may bring particular clarity to the question and may even give a clue to the answer.

Once upon a time — among an ancient people — an only child of a family of thread makers was orphaned. Wandering nomad weavers took the boy into their tribe for awhile but, for lack of means, eventually had to sell him as an apprentice to a family of shipbuilders. In their situation, the shipbuilders trained him to make masts. Mastmaking was a good trade, in very great demand in this sailing town.

The young man liked the work; but years later, while on a business voyage for the mastmakers, this same young man — once an orphaned spinner, once an abandoned weaver and now a satisfied

mastmaker — was shipwrecked on a primitive is-
land.

And in this place the people lived in wait for the ful-
fillment of a promise that God would some day send a
foreigner who would help them save their religious
treasures from ruin by the hostile environment. All
other foreigners were to be rejected.

"Are you the one for whom we wait? Are you the one
who will save our religious treasure?" they asked.

"At that very moment the young man understood
both his past and his future. He took the memory of
his experience as a spinner of thread and made rope;
he took the memory of his experience as a weaver and
made cloth; he took the memory of his experience as a
mastmaker and made long, strong, poles. And out of
all these memories, he fashioned the vision of a tent
which saved the values of that people.

The point is that memory and vision are of a piece. Each without the other is an orphan. The question for religious leaders of
our day is not simply how shall we teach or what shall we teach.
The question is both how shall we teach and what shall we teach
if religion is to make a difference in our own time. Because once
again, religion has never been more important to the future of
the world.

Why? In the first place, the total world situation has shifted.
Strong and isolated national entities are now shadows of the
past and have given way to the global village. Human isolation
has faded into human unity whether we want it or not, whether
we deal with it well or not. Every single segment of humanity is
now linked, forever. We're linked through travel; the Concord
races between Dulles and Europe in four hours, the same time it
takes a train to go from Washington to New York City. We're
linked through communication; we don't have to go places to see

and learn new things because satellites ring the planet and make contact instant and universal. Most of all, as a people we're linked through interdependence. Each of us draws from the same resource pool — and some of us draw more than others. The linkage is not mere academic speculation; it is the present world reality. We must relate. We have no choice.

In the second place, the center of the world is shifting. Population and youth and need are all now loading toward the Third World, and with them the momentum for change. Iran and Iraq, Africa and China, Latin America and Asia all look toward the power and the profits of the West with some dismay and some resentment. Every day the Christians of the West are looked at with more scrutiny and more suspicion and more disdain.

The question is not: What is a Christian? The question is: Does being a Christian make any difference for good in a world staggering under the weight of inequity? In a world whose agenda will stress the development of the undeveloped, the social needs of societies in need, and the common good of all the people rather than the singular good of a few particular peoples, what kind of difference does American Christianity make? Indeed the question: What does it mean to be a religious leader today, an emphasis on vision or a dedication to memory, has perhaps never been more important.

As I struggled with this question, I found myself returning again and again to two perspectives: The first comes from a story of a farm town out West that was facing drought.

The summer had been particularly hot and unrelenting; the crops were literally burning up; the soil had gone to powder; the streams were dry. The local church wanted to do its civic best to ease the situation so the pastor called an emergency prayer meeting. He said to the congregation's wise old deacon:

"Brother John, you've been long years in this church; you're holy and close to God. We're now asking you to lead this congregation in prayer to move the Lord to send us rain." And the deacon got up in the midst of the congregation and said, " 'Taint no use praying for rain. . . ."

The pastor was shocked. "Have you lost your faith, old man?" he asked. "Are you telling us after all these years that you don't believe in prayer?"

And the old man said, "It's got nothin' to do with believing in prayer. Of course I believe in prayin'. I'm just trying to tell you that it's no use prayin' for rain when the wind is coming from the wrong direction."

The message is clear: hard facts have to be faced, even in religion.

But then I remembered a second perspective that was even more challenging than the first. The story reads:

On a roadside outside the village an old Sufi master knelt searching in the dust.

"Master," the people asked as they passed by, "what are you doing?"

"I have lost the treasure of my life," the old man said, "and I am searching for it."

So, one after the other, people got down in the dust of the road to help. Finally, as the sun rose higher and higher in the sky and the hot day wore on, someone finally asked, "Master, are you sure you lost your treasure here?"

The master replied, "Oh, no, I didn't lose it here. I lost my treasure on the other side of the mountain."

"But if you lost your treasure over there," they said, "why are you looking over here?"

And the master answered, "I'm looking over here because there's more light here."

The perspectives are clear; the learning is obvious: hard facts, to be understood, often have to be looked at from new and fresh perspectives.

The problem for the church today is that we have some hard facts to indicate that we, too, are losing some religious treasures. Past studies of religion in America — the Stark-Glock Studies of 1970 and the Gallup research between 1950-1980, for example — defined three significant trends in contemporary American religious thought.

The Stark-Glock study reported that we were undergoing a major shift in belief among American Christians. Orthodox and traditional tenets about the supernatural — the idea of a personal God, the concept of a divine Savior, the notion of eternal life — were eroding among people under fifty in every Christian denomination.

But the study also reported that this massive change of belief could not be characterized as transition from belief to unbelief, but that it was actually a transition from one form of belief to another. It was a shift from the mystical to the ethical; from rejection of private vices to a sense of social sin. It was a shift from preparation for the next life to the realization that there is an obligation to build the kingdom of God on earth, here and now.

The study concluded that if Church leaders did not recognize the situation, the church would drift, lose influence, and provide at best only psychic comfort for the psychologically weak.

Then over a period of twenty years, the Princeton Religion Research Center published *Religion in America,* a series of updated reports on American religious life and thought that confirmed all the other data. These studies found that 90 percent of the people said they believed in God; 90 percent said they prayed; 90 percent said they wanted religious education and religious training for their children.

But fewer than half said they had confidence in organized religion, any organized religion. And sure enough, membership had declined; Sunday attendance had dropped drastically (to less than half of previous rates); church support had decreased significantly.

In 1952, 75 percent of the young people in the United States (those between the ages of 18 and 24) said religion was the most important influence in their lives. But by 1980, less than one-third of that same age group (30 percent of the 18-24 year olds in this country) were still willing to say that religion was the most important motivator in their lives.

Indeed we have hard facts to indicate that we are losing some of our religious treasure, and not in a period of affluence and order, but in a period of massive starvation, a period of unprecedented economic exploitation of entire peoples, of blatant denial of human rights, in a period of the very real threat of planetary holocaust.

Where is religious leadership here? Where are memory and vision?

We have, perhaps, like the farm town never needed accurate understanding more or, like the Sufi, never needed fresher perspective more. In 1983, the Ecumenical and Cultural Research Center in Collegeville, Minnesota, published *Faith and Ferment,* a $200,000 ecumenical interdisciplinary study of the nature of religious belief in contemporary, church-going Christianity. And the new data are equally clear: Christians of all denominations were very like one another in their responses. They were divided among themselves in significant proportions over whether or not the Bible is the verbatim Word of God to be interpreted literally, or an authoritative guide to wisdom and righteousness that is to be given place and privilege.

They questioned among themselves in significant proportions whether or not sexual ethics as we knew them in the past were really a given. They questioned in what way justice — as well as charity — was a mandate of the Christian dispensation. They questioned exactly how Christians have ethical responsibility for corporate integrity; when and where sexism and racism are sinful; what kinds of war and which political and economic theories are moral. They struggled over whether or not technology is really subject to morality; whether or not Christians ought to ask whether what is technically possible is also morally appropriate.

Almost three-fourths of them said that the teaching of their Church on war is unclear. Almost half said that they simply didn't know whether Christianity has anything to do with the economic standards of a society or not. And almost all said that "There does not exist among you slave or free, Jew or Greek, male or female" (Gal. 3:18) meant that there must be no discrimination in the Church.

But as the issues became more and more specified, Christian support and certainty deteriorated rapidly. For they said in large numbers (76-85 percent) that both charity and justice were the proper concerns of the Church and that the Church should work to make them possible — until they were confronted with actual situations:

- Should the church work for the rights of the elderly in society? Over two-thirds said yes.

- Should the church work for the rights of minorities in society? Only one-half were as convinced;

- Should the church work for the rights of women in the church?
Less than one-half were able to agree;

- Should the church work for the rights of women in society? Just two-fifths were as committed to this as they were to concern for the elderly.

Morality, it seems may be a function of convenience in a world that is crushingly inconvenient for many.

The cleavage becomes even sharper on other questions. Ask: Should the church give full support to any war? Almost half of those born before Hiroshima said yes, but less than one quarter of those born after Hiroshima agree. Ask: Should the United States attain military superiority? A firm 40 percent of those born before Hiroshima said yes; but less than 20 percent of those born after Hiroshima felt the same. Worse, perhaps, older people — people born before Hiroshima — said that the principles of Christianity were an answer to world problems. Younger people — people who have seen what we have done with our "principles" — said they were not.

Older people said the mission of the church was to convert. Younger people said that the mission of the church was to influence and to model; to practice what we preach, perhaps.

Clearly old absolutes are blurring in our time. Whole new areas of thought call for exploration; vast areas of old concepts call for redefinition in the Christian community. But they call for modeling, as well. Surely contemporary religious leaders bear some great responsibility for that. The philosopher says: Those who have lived well for their own time have lived well for all time.

For the sake of the future, what does the present demand of religious leadership today? The answer, I believe, depends on a model of Christian memory that is not measured by the most mediocre moments of faith. The answer depends on a model of Christian vision that does not vacillate between the morally imperative and the socially acceptable. In these times, to be true to the trust of "religious leadership" we need to take Esther as a model of the memory of the church and Mary Magdalene as a model of its vision.

Think of Esther for a moment. Who was she? What did she do? Esther was the chosen woman of a fallen race. Her people were in danger of extinction; they held notions strange and dangerous to the officials of that place. Her people believed in the power of God over all powers. Her people believed in the dignity of creation above all dignities, in the essential, inviolable, demanding humanity of all human beings. But Esther herself was safe and favored and successful. She had come up in the world, in fact. She had accepted the system; she had gone along with things, and as a result came out of the Jewish ghetto as queen to the foreigner king. But powerless nevertheless, she figured. The king made the decrees, after all. He hand-picked his advisors. He limited information and targeted enemies.

His world-view was completely other than hers. What could they possibly expect from her? She was just a functionary in the system. But Mordechai, — the one whose life was threatened, the one on whose back prejudice had fallen heavily, the one for whom life was not blessing but curse, the one who looked to her for help because of her background — insisted: "Remember who you are! Remember who you are. Whatever the cost, remember who you are!"

And finally the vigor and depth of her past made her capable of a dangerous present. "I will go to the king," she finally answered Mordechai, "whether he calls me or not. And if I perish, I perish."

Today's church needs the memory of Esther. Today's church holds the gospel of the beatitudes in a world where the blessings of security, of sufficiency, of safety, are the birthright of the rich and powerful but the burdens of the poor. In today's church it is you and I who are the safe, the favored, the successful ones. You and I are the ones who have come up in the world, who have moved out of the ghettos of 1850 and 1900 and 1940 America to college, to two-car garages, to callousness. We really believe, you and I, that if we did it, and our grandparents did it, and our uncles did it, well then anyone can do it if they really want to and have the stamina for it and the character for it and the quality for it.

But listen! Today, Mordechai the black, Mordechai the woman, Mordechai the Hispanic, Mordechai the Ethiopian, Mordechai the Russian, Mordechai the Latin-American, Mordechai the old, Mordechai the unemployed is calling again and to us, too: "Remember who you are! Remember who you are!"

Remember that today people look to us, as the professionals of the church, to be a sign that the church that stood with the Indians, the church that stood with the immigrants, the church that stood with the trade unionists, the church that stood with the poor through the depression for just legislation and just distribution of goods and just access to the centers of power, — that that Church stands again, through us, with the new poor and the new powerless and the newly-oppressed.

"Remember the day of your lowly estate," Mordechai wrote to Esther. "If you now remain silent, relief and deliverance will come to the people from another source, but you and your house will perish. Who knows but perhaps it was for just such a time as this that you came to this throne."

Yes, religious leaders, the church of our time needs the memory of Esther. In a time of danger and moral darkness we, too, have a past that compels us.

But memory is not enough. The past is a standard for the present but it must not be its plague and it cannot be its pitch. Memory does not guarantee vision; vision is a function of the gospel told over and over again.

Religious leadership in our time needs conviction as well as content; courage as well as compassion; principle as well as precept. It needs vision as well as memory.

But what will the vision be? Christianity is clearly at a crossover moment in history; confusion is obviously deep and pervasive. How shall we deal with the future?

Esther was the chosen woman of a fallen race who confronted an imperfect present not with the practices of the past but with its principles, but Mary Magdalene was the fallen woman of a chosen race who confronted an imperfect present not with the precepts of the past but with the power of its prophetic vision.

Mary Magdalene had the vision in her time to follow Jesus from Jew to Gentile, from mainstream to marginal, in the very face of the disapproval from the powerful of both the church and the state. Mary Magdalene had the vision it took to stand at the cross of this revolutionary whose crime was a bias for the poor, when being there in public and recognized risked her own security. Mary Magdalene had the vision it took to go on following and ministering all the way to the tomb. Mary Magdalene had the prophetic vision it took to proclaim what no one, not even the apostles, believed.

Mary Magdalene recognized possibility in the midst of the imperfect and proclaimed it despite the rejection of the public, despite the pressure from the officials, despite the risk to her own future, despite the incredulity of those who could have and should have believed. Mary Magdalene called the present beyond the past. And today Mary Magdalene calls all of us, too, beyond memory to vision.

We talk religion in a world where half the human race is in bondage to the other half. We catechize in a world where the messages to women that they are inferior are very clear. We catechize, you and I, in a world where one-third of the women in the labor force are the sole supporters of their families, but where working women with college degrees earn an average of $2200 less per year than males who dropped out of high school.

We catechize in a world where a woman receives a lesser portion of her husband's social security payment after he dies despite the fact that if she dies first he will still receive the total amount. The message is very clear: Say what you want about how much we value motherhood and how wonderful it is for women to stay in the home, but when all is said and done, the money is obviously his, not theirs, and she will be left to fend for herself in her old age with only half of a pension to count on. And as religious leaders we say nothing. We "practice our religion" in a world where, as a result, two-thirds of the poor are women. "Blessed are the poor," we preach and then we do nothing for women.

We teach religion in a world where 100 percent of the women of the world will be annihilated in the nuclear wars that men design to "protect them" and where no one will even bother to ask the women if that's all right. We teach religion in a world where women are left out of even the language in their own church. But what is worse, we teach religion in a world where people say God wants it that way.

What vision will the religious leaders of our time bring to sexism?

We talk religion while people die of hunger. We teach the catechism while our own country exports its factories, but not its wages or its working conditions or its medical benefits, to the poor of other nations. We catechize in a country where for every $84 of military supplies we give in foreign aid we give only $2.00 in economic help. We then tell ourselves how beneficent we are to the poor of the world, even though no one can live in a bullet or wear a bomber or feed their children a tank.

What vision will the religious leaders of our time bring to American foreign policy and economics?

We teach the love of Jesus in a country that claims that its only role in the arms race is deterrence but which developed eight of the world's nine present nuclear weapons systems first. We teach the love of Jesus in a country which has, according to the Pentagon Papers published in the *Monthly Review* (October 1983), threatened the use of nuclear force nine times since 1945 for political reasons, six of those nine times against totally nonnuclear nations. We talk about religious leadership in the only nation that has ever used atomic force, not once but twice.

But it isn't so much that we catechize in a country where the balance of terror is holding the world hostage to fear. We are catechizing in a country that has already begun to turn nuclear war against itself.

People are out of work in this country today, the government says, because the American factory system is obsolete. But instead of using tax dollars to rebuild the industrial system of the United States, we are blindly building bombs. People are out of work despite the availability of new technology because they have not been trained for its use. But instead of updating the educational system of this country, we are blindly making missiles to defend a decrepit one.

People who have worked all their lives in this country fear their old age because health care, housing, gas, oil and electricity costs — the very basics of life — are raging out of sight in the United States of America. But instead of developing human service programs or new resources, we are blindly spending the money of the poor on sinister submarines, the purpose of which is to stalk the poor of other nations.

Five and a half billion dollars of the 1982 $187 billion military budget (or simply two less nuclear-powered aircraft carriers) could have restored all education monies and the CETA training programs that were cut from the budget that year. One and three-quarter billion dollars of the 1982 $187 billion military budget (or just one less Trident submarine) could have restored the entire food stamp program. Eleven billion dollars of the 1982 $187 billion military budget (or the elimination of the Cruise missile program which adds absolutely nothing to our present defense system but a trip-switch to terror) could have restored all the subsidized housing for the elderly, the poor, and the handicapped which was cut from the budget that year.

And while we have religion classes, the government cuts more and more from the lives of the people we call neighbor. They cut funds from Job Corps, from education, from farmers, from small business administration, from rural development, from museums and art galleries and all under the guise of "defense." And this despite the fact that everyone now knows, including the Pentagon, that if we ever detonate even less than 1 percent of our present nuclear arsenal, we will plunge the entire world into a dark, cold, radioactive winter for over a year whether anyone ever retaliates or not.

The question is not how many times we may morally prepare to destroy the world. The question for religious leaders of our time is: Isn't once enough? We refuse to be a welfare state; we have chosen instead to be a warfare state — and we see little moral denunciation of that by religious leaders today.

What vision will these leaders bring to American military policy?

We talk religion in a world that worships the bread but does not distribute it; that practices ritual rather than righteousness; that confesses but does not repent. In religious education, textbooks and exercises and teachers are for times of peace. We have need for prophets now. The catechism is not enough in our time; only the gospel will do.

We need the memory of Esther and the vision of Mary Magdalene when we are told: "This is an imperfect world; you just have to get used to it. That's the way things are."

Religious leaders need the memory of Esther and the vision of Mary Magdalene when they are told that they imagine the ideal and phantasize the impossible.

The Church needs the memory of Esther and the vision of Mary Magdalene when they say to us: "What you want can't be done."

The obstacles to catechesis in this world are obvious. Civil religion, the notion that God's will and the American dream are one and the same thing, is anti-gospel in a suffering world. Institutionalism, the notion that if there is a religious education program there must be religious education, is just a panacea in a suffering world. Symbolism, the notion that practices and pietisms are sufficient substitutes for Christianity, is an empty sign of religion in a suffering world. Privatism, an emphasis on personal rather than social sin, is only half the gospel in a suffering world.

We need the memory of Esther. We need the vision of Mary Magdalene.

For it is essential to remember that memory is simply not enough. Jean Francois Steiner's now classic account of human behavior in the Jewish concentration camp of Treblinka gives a sobering focus to our own lives as religious leaders. The Germans, Steiner tells us, found it very inconvenient to work with a perpetually inexperienced labor force so they established a set of longer-term workers who would be sent to the gas chambers only after an extended period of time. And the Jews cooperated. They developed "relationships" with their masters. They formed a prison orchestra that played as fellow prisoners were being brought to the execution site. They developed camp entertainment: a boxing ring, a park and a zoo, even a cabaret. Indeed, they helped to dispose of the bodies of their own brothers and sisters. And they put off revolt until it was too late, hoping their time would not run out. They made calculations: the original Jewish population of Warsaw, the thousands that had come to the camp, the numbers that must be left. They feared risk; they didn't want to draw disfavor on themselves, and in their hearts they really felt that they would outlive the crisis. No time seemed the right time to refuse to continue the madness. The Jews at Treblinka had turned an atrocious situation into the normal and in the end they all perished. The people of Treblinka had memory — but a memory without vision.

Both Esther and Mary Magdalene had proclaimed the impossible in the face of the impossible. In our time, we too are now quietly turning an atrocious situation into the normal; and for us, too, the time is running out. If the gospel is to be proclaimed in our age we simply cannot go on, you and I, as religious leaders doing business as usual, hoping against hope that the gospel will come without our having to do something to change our own lives to bring it about. Like Esther and Mary Magdalene, you and I are forever burdened. We live knowing that the mark of religion in the present is whether or not the future will be different because of us.

The Hasidic masters tell a tale of an old teacher who ran through the streets of the city shouting: "Power, greed, and corruption; power, greed, and corruption."

One day a child asked him: "Rabbi, don't you realize that no one is listening to you?"

"Oh, I know that," the teacher said.

"Then why do you go on shouting," the child said, "if nothing changes?"

"You don't understand," the rabbi said. "I don't shout in order to change them; I shout so that they cannot change me."

In a world where, as Camus says, the saints of our time are those who refuse to be either its executioners or its victims, my prayer is that our religious leaders will be and do and shout, both the memory and the vision of the church, for the sake of the suffering, for the sake of the children, for the sake of the world.

5. HIROSHIMA REMEMBERED NEW, AUGUST 6, 1985

Two scriptures challenge our authenticity forever; two scriptures dictate what this generation's answer to Hiroshima must be. One is from the Hebrew Testament of Western culture and one from Sufi religious literature of the East.

In the West, Deuteronomy cries out in the face of Hiroshima:

> I call heaven and earth today to witness against you: I have set before you life and death, a blessing and a curse. Choose life that you and your descendants might live.

Then in the tales of the Sufi Masters we read about a woman with a similar concern:

> "Where can I find the tree of life?" she asked the Holy One.
>
> "You would be best advised to study with me," the Holy One said, "But if you will not do so, you will have to travel resolutely and at times restlessly thoughout the world."
>
> But the woman had no patience for waiting to see what would grow from what had already been planted and so she left him for another.
>
> First she went to the scientists, then to the military leaders, then to the heads of government, then to the wealthy of the kingdom, and to many, many more but

to no avail. Among them they offered only potions that sickened, and weapons that killed, and profits that eroded, and power that blinded. Never life.

She passed forty years in that search until finally she came back again to that garden in her own village. And there stood the Tree and from its branches hung the bright fruit of life. Standing beside the Tree was the Holy One she had met 40 years before.

"Why did you not tell me when we first met that you were the keeper of the Tree of Life?" she asked him.

"Because you would not have believed me then," the Holy One answered. "And besides, the tree produces fruit only once every 40 years."

And the woman began to dance!

Two lessons: First, readiness, it seems, has something to do with choosing life; secondly, only life breeds life.

Every day I, too, get the chance to choose life. Every day the letters pour across my desk. Good letters, sincere letters: Send this postcard to Congress. Give money to support this group. Fill out this survey. Call this Federal office to protest apartheid or starvation or militarism. And, dutifully, I fill out a few of the cards and manage to make at least some of the telephone calls and send my single dollar bill in the hope that they really mean it when they say that every contribution counts no matter how small. But, morning after morning, the headlines stay the same.

We're still trying to destabilize the government of Nicaragua.

We're still militarizing the government of El Salvador.

We're still building billions of dollars worth of new missiles that we don't need, or putting them into vulnerable launching sites where, in order not to lose them, we will have to use them first.

We still lie about Russian-American nuclear parity and demonize the enemy by pointing out that they have more land-based nuclear weapons than we have but failing to explain that we have deliberately chosen to put two-thirds of our nuclear attack strategy into bombers and submarines which the Soviets, by and large, do not have.

We still breed hate and fear in the citizenry to justify the continued economic link between the political-military-industrial complex of this country.

We still go on preparing for the next Hiroshima. Of course the situation will go on. Because there are those who have decreed it so and few who resist. In fact, in the light of this terrible anniversary, I have tried to think of one oppressive or sinful or misguided government that ever changed itself without pressure from the people. The French did not. The English did not. The Vietnamese did not. The czarist regimes of Russia did not. No. The fact is that it took revolution in every case.

The pride of American history is that the government is responsive to the people. And there is plenty of proof of that: Pressure from the people ended slavery; pressure from the people secured the labor unions; pressure from the people achieved the vote for women; pressure from the people ended the Vietnam War.

Americans marched in the streets for these changes and the changes came. Not without effort and not without sacrifice, but come they did. If the people lead, we learned, eventually the leaders will follow. Today, however, few Americans march in the streets against nuclear holocaust. Only a couple against apartheid. Few, if any, because of the poor or the hungry or the unemployed or the use of resources for the high art of destruction rather than for human development.

Now, forty years after Hiroshima, it is time to ask: Whose fault is the arms race anyway? Maybe it's about time that we stop blaming the current President and look to what it is that keeps the American people, you and me, from choosing life. What is it that keeps us, like the seeker in the Sufi tale, looking for it in the wrong places? What is it that keeps us so apparently satisfied with a system that rapes our resources and poisons our environment and threatens the lives of our children — and their children?

Maybe we have to ask what it is about this sin of death that has seduced us as a people and held us for forty long years while Hiroshima stands mute and waiting for our response, for our repentance, for the radical recommitment of this nation to life. Is it fear that keeps us on the road to military madness? Is it the thought of hordes of Russian Tartars sweeping across the country? Is it fear of a primitive people — so barbarian, so half-human — that no reasonable defense is possible, to whose onslaught only planetary suicide is an acceptable response?

But if it's fear of them, how account for our apparent lack of fear of our own reactions? After all, we are the ones who have already used the atomic bomb, not once, but twice when — recently released government documents tell us — we knew that Japan had already asked for peace; that the bomb was not necessary to end the war; that a demonstration of its power was at least questionable.

And we are the ones who now make plans to use it again; who refuse to say that we will not use it first. We are the ones who used an atomic bomb on a population largely non-combatant and civilian, not on military installations. For the city of Hiroshima was no military installation; Hiroshima was a city full of old men and children and women. We are the ones who used two different atomic weapons at the same time in order to experiment, knowing after the release of the first one that there was simply no possible military response to so monstrous an act.

Who really ought to fear whom? Maybe the most significant thing we have to do on this fortieth anniversary of Hiroshima is to admit that possibly, just possibly, deterrence may be what they build against us, not what we build against them. Is it powerlessness that leads us to forego life? Are we quiet — quiescent — in the face of the nuclear vacuum because we know that there is simply nothing else that we can do? Is it because, secretly, we feel that our system does not work nearly as well as we like to say it does? Is it because we know that the high and the mighty will not listen, as they are not listening to the anti-nuclear protestors in England and Belgium and Holland and New Zealand because it suits them not to? Or is it because the people, too, want the jobs — few as they are — that come with the contracts; that the people, too, want the money that comes from the bases without the effort of converting the economy to make our money in more humane ways?

Indeed, if powerlessness is the issue, then what becomes of the American self-image of democratic keeper of the world? Is it hopelessness that militates against our choice of life in a time of death? Is it the notion that there is no stopping this thing; that someone somewhere will someday push the ultimate button and that we are already well beyond the point of no return?

But if that is the case, how did we get there? Isn't it good, decent Americans — people like you and me — who have elected the politicians, paid the taxes, wheedled the contracts, worked on the nuclear assembly lines, and debated and upheld the balance-of-terror policies that now hold the entire world hostage to fear?

No, I submit that it may be none of these things. Fear and powerlessness and hopelessness are specious arguments, lame excuses for choosing death rather than life. I think instead that it is simply individualism gone aground. Individualism, in fact, may be more the fault line of present civilization than nuclear weaponry. We may as a people have gone as far as we can go confusing individualism and personal responsibility. Individualism and personal responsibility are not synonyms.

Individualism says, "Those problems are not my problems," and withdraws into isolation. Personal responsibility says, "If any people have a problem, it is my problem, too," and bends itself to change things. In an individualistic world, an atomized society which teaches "Everybody for themselves" has created an atomic world that threatens, ironically, to destroy all of us together.

If we can risk nuclear war, surely we ought to be able to risk a nuclear freeze. But people hardly even seem to notice the question; not its contradictions, not its urgency, because individualism has taught us — false teacher that it is — that this is really not our problem. We have to trust the government, we say. We have to rely on the people who know about these things, on the people whose responsibility it is to try to deal with them, in the office or the Congress or the church. It's their problem, not mine. If my world is comfortable and my job is safe, the individualist says, then God's in the heavens, all's right with the world. Individualism may be a terminal disease that renders humanity blind, deaf and dumb.

Louis XV, King of France prior to the French Revolution, suffered from the same kind of sickness. "After me, the deluge," he boasted and went on living in the style to which he had become accustomed, until, of course, it and his entire world with it were destroyed by the very demon he had himself let grow.

Individualism is no response to a telephone call from Hiroshima; only personal responsibility will do. Time after time, people across the country march in small group after small group in demonstrations for peace. Yesterday in Washington they tied a ribbon around the Pentagon as a record of what they will most miss in a nuclear war. Time after time a few are arrested for praying within the temple precincts of the God of War: in the White House, at the State Department, outside the HEW Building, in front of the Russian Embassy, near the Embassy of South Africa. The question is, why are there so few? Why is so little attention paid to peace rallies like tonight's, to people like you? Why do they seem to accomplish so little? Hopelessness? Fear? Powerlessness? I doubt it. It might be, I'm afraid, that endemic, rampant individualism is really the problem. The real problem may simply be that I have sent one card too few, given one dollar too little, failed to speak out one more time, loved issues rather than life, and waited, hoping against hope to outlive the crisis.

Forty years ago in our lifetime, like the woman in the Sufi tale, our nation came to a crossroads. In our search for knowledge and power the answers from the Holy One disappointed: "Choose life; stay with me; obey my commands. If you choose other gods you will perish."

The advent of the nuclear age disguised as the Tree of Life with its fruits of knowledge and power and profit and prestige were too tempting. Already the ashes of Hiroshima and Nagasaki were ample proof of knowledge without limit and power without price. But to see it was not to know its force, not to realize its impact, not to fear its growth. The world that unleashed it has been disappointed in its promise. The force that promised peace has brought oppression; the knowledge that conquered nature is not benign; the magic that muted conflict gives no solution; and as a people we have closed our eyes to the chaos of our own creating. What we made impossible, we continue to pursue: knowledge without conscience and power without compassion. We look to governments to protect us, having made protection impossible. We look to science to enlighten us and refuse to face its darkness. We look to soldiers to set us free and become enslaved to the military.

Yes, the Sufi master teaches us that life is within our grasp and that nothing less will suffice, that anything else will destroy, that readiness and openness and vision are essential to new life. Yes, the Sufi master teaches us what it is to fail to find the Tree of Life in our midst and to look and lust for it in lying lips and bloody deeds. But the Sufi master teaches, too, that truth blooms every 40 years.

Here tonight we are observing a fortieth anniversary of death. Again, heaven and earth are summoned to bear witness against us. Tomorrow, our choices can alter again the course of the universe. It is possible now that a deliberate refusal to choose life will mean not only an end to life on earth but will usher in the destruction of our planetary system. The stakes are staggering, our resources meager. But the Book of Deuteronomy teaches that life is possible. And the Sufi agrees. The choice is ours. We have simply to choose it and to go on choosing day after day, single decision after single decision, as singularly small as each decision may seem.

Let us each choose to do what we can to save the future. Let us choose personal responsibility over individualism so that tomorrow morning the whole world can be free of fear. Today let us choose life so that tomorrow, with the Sufi woman, we and the world with us can dance and dance and dance in a wonderously absurd and wild affirmation of the victory of life over death.

The future of the planet, the world, and the nation may well depend on our doing what only we can: In the face of the policies of death, we must choose life. And choose. And choose. And choose.

6. NO TIME FOR NICODEMUS: A STUDY IN MORAL IMPERATIVES

One night a young rabbi dreamed that he had been taken to a great place which he automatically presumed was heaven. And there this ardent student of the Covenant was permitted to approach what was presumably the temple of Paradise where the sages of the Talmud were spending eternal life. But what he saw there was that the sages were simply sitting around studying the Talmud. And the young disciple was very disappointed and thought, "Is this all there is to heaven?" Then suddenly he heard a voice, "You are mistaken. The sages are not in Paradise. Paradise is in the sages."

The question for Catholic education today is still the same.

What will our students say of us: "I had teachers who taught about Paradise" or "Paradise was in my teachers"?

It is out of that perspective that one scriptural image arises to confront Catholic education in a special way at this period of our history. The figure is the Pharisee Nicodemus, an important character for religious educators today because Nicodemus is a study, a challenge, a paradigm, and a warning to us all.

In the first place, Nicodemus was a religious figure to the Jews. He was good stock. He believed in the system and the system believed in him. Nicodemus had respectability; he was one of those pillar-of-the-church types.

In the second place, Nicodemus was a teacher — "THE Teacher," the Greek text says. Consequently, Nicodemus had credibility because he was schooled in the Law; he was a professional believer.

In the third place, Nicodemus was an establishment presence in Jesus' otherwise rag-tag ministry. Most of the others who followed Jesus were rabble or outcasts or the working class or the poor. But Nicodemus was somebody with influence. He was a person of sound judgment, of high moral principles, a leader in the Jewish community. What people like Nicodemus said meant something.

And those are precisely the problems. For this believer, this leader, this pillar-of-the-church did very little.

Nicodemus went to Jesus only at night; he asked questions he should have known the answers to; after all, he was a Pharisee, not a Sadducee. He believed in eternal life and the Kingdom of God.

Nicodemus attempted to move his own system in Jesus' behalf only once and then feebly. Nicodemus asked what he should do in order to be saved. But when he was told he had to begin all over again, Nicodemus went away.

After that, we see Nicodemus only once more. Nicodemus appears in secret again to bury Jesus and spends a lot of money doing it. Although it is true that what people like Nicodemus said meant something, the problem is that Nicodemus said so little to the people about the great issues of his time.

Nicodemus is the conscience of all of us who are religious figures, teachers, establishment people. We too have respectability, credibility and influence. And we must also in this time, in this place, in this world go down into the womb and be born again if Catholic education is to maintain the commitment to freedom and peace out of which it stems.

Catholic education has at its very base a commitment to free-dom and a call to peace. One hundred years ago Catholic educa-tion in this country did not tolerate the self-fulfilling prophecy of prejudice against Catholics or domination by the government or the exclusion of a major portion of its citizens from the sys-tem. Instead, Catholic education built the cry for freedom and peace right into the very fabric of this country. It prepared scores of foreign-speaking immigrant children to take their place in a white, Anglo-Saxon, Protestant society that preached democracy but practiced separatism, that promised equal op-portunity but promoted anti-Catholicism, that talked indi-vidualism but expected assimilation. In that world, a hundred years ago, there were only two types of people: Catholics and Protestants. The task was to establish the Church, to win a place for the people in the culture. In this environment, Catholic education and Catholic educators did just that: they scraped and struggled and sacrificed themselves to preserve the faith in a Protestant environment and to insert the faithful into a closed society. With the accession of John F. Kennedy to the presidency of the United States, that task was largely accomplished.

Our task is a new one. Between that world and this, a whole world view has changed and with it the role of religious educa-tion. We must teach now with all our hearts, not because the Church is under siege but because the world is under siege. We teach now not for a Church without rights but for whole peoples without rights: not because the Church is in danger but because the very planet is in danger. In the early days of Catholic educa-tion, a parochial church in an insular world needed to educate for literacy, for life-skills, for liturgy, for language. Now in this time, an ecumenical church in an interdependent world must educate for people over machines, for planet over profit, for pur-pose over power, for prophecy over piety.

There is no time for Nicodemus now. There is no time for the silent, the stealthy, the safe. We need teachers who do not sim-ply talk about the Gospel; we need teachers who will live it. We can no longer afford good Catholic leadership; what we need now is great Catholic leadership. This is what Catholic education gave to the social questions of the past: to discrimination, to labor problems, to pluralism. And that is what Catholic educators must give to the great social questions of the present if Catholic education is to maintain its credibility, keep its quality, and make its contribution to secure a better world. But those who set out to teach freedom and peace in the context of Catholicism need to give special thought to exactly what that means. Nothing in Scripture leads us to believe that teaching peace and maintaining freedom is a comfortable thing:

- Jeremiah ran through the streets naked to get people's attention.

- Esther faced death for her people but went uninvited to the king.

- Moses was run out of town.

No, the Scripture is sure proof that standing for freedom and pressing for peace has nothing to do with getting promoted, fitting in, being establishment, being approved, being safe. The question is: How can we know what it means to maintain freedom and build the peace in our time? And then, how can teachers teach it?

The answer is not in Nicodemus.

The answer, I think, is at the healing pool at Bethsaida. Bethsaida is really where Catholic educators need to go to discover what makes for both freedom and peace in our time, because Bethsaida is a lesson in faith and obedience. Bethsaida was one of those moments on the edge of life, a breakthrough, breakdown world of turmoil and peace. It was a place of both poverty and prosperity, of freedom and enslavement, of haves and have-nots, of self-defense and destruction, of great promise and greater threat.

Great things happened at Bethsaida; but tragic things happened there, too. And all for the same reason: Bethsaida is a place alive with possibility and the power of it, but Bethsaida is also heavy with the oppressiveness of possibility unfulfilled. And that's what Nicodemus, what Americans, what Catholic educators dedicated to freedom and searching for peace have to understand. Breakthroughs happened at Bethsaida. Not everything was bad there. "Every year" Scripture reads, "the waters stir and those who get there first are healed." For all the others, though, Bethsaida breaks down hope, breaks down promise, breaks down freedom and peace. Until Jesus comes, walking purposefully through the rushing, running, striving crowd; among the blind, over the lame, around the paralyzed. And he goes not to the waters but straight up the hill to the far edge of the crowd, to one who hasn't walked upright his whole adult life, to one who has been overlooked, pushed down, pushed out of the stream of life here, year after year after year. "Don't you want to be healed?" Jesus asks. And the forgotten one answers not "Yes," not "No," not "My turn is coming." The paralytic answers simply: "Sir, there is no one to carry me down!"

And what does the teacher teach here? After all, the paralytic had had his chance. The situation is very clear. That's the way the system is. Some people just don't have the know-how, the gumption, the natural ability, the character it takes to get ahead. Some people are just inherently lazy or essentially evil, just fundamentally dishonest, naturally inept. Some people can't get freedom; some people don't deserve peace. There are rules, policies, circumstances, and ideologies to be considered. To violate the Sabbath, to tamper with cultural expectations can do more harm than good. After all, it's been thirty-eight years. To wait a little longer, to be a little patient, to do the thing right surely can't be asking too much.

The point is that what happens at Bethsaida doesn't depend on the paralytic but on the faith-life of the teacher. It's what the teacher believes that faith demands in this situation that makes

Bethsaida either a breakthrough or a breakdown place.

The history of spirituality identifies three basic faith responses that can be brought to the paralytic at Bethsaida.

The first is intellectualist. An intellectualist faith is concerned about knowing God and mystical illumination. The problem is that intellectual faith often lacks commitment to the earthly city. The intellectualist at Bethsaida says to the paralytic, "This situation is God's will for you; it will make you very close to God if you just offer it up." The intellectualist teaches that the Church is primarily a set of doctrines, a range of beliefs, a type of institution to be maintained. The intellectualist talks a lot about faith and waits for union with God.

The second thread in the spiritual history of the nature of faith is relational or personalist. The teacher whose faith is personalist looks to the personal beneficence of God and is a very devotional person. The personalist at Bethsaida says a rosary or reads a book on the meditations of the sufferings of Christ and sits down with the paralytic to wait for the waters to stir next year. Personalists teach about building community and talk a lot about love.

A third dimension of the nature of faith in the history of spirituality is performative. The one who believes that faith is performative believes that the Gospel is only fully taught when the Word becomes transforming action. Performative faith is a commitment to upbuilding the kingdom by establishing on earth a just society out of which peace and freedom come. Teachers whose faith is performative want Nicodemus to begin again and again and again for as long as it takes to free us from a mentality of the enemy being the other, to begin again as long as it takes to win the peace rather than start the war.

Teachers who teach a performative faith are "Our Father" people who pray daily "Thy kingdom come; Thy will be done" and then do something to bring it about. For those whose faith is performative the Church is servant. The servant Church goes to

Bethsaida not simply to give testimony or a talk or simply to be a warm presence. The servant Church goes to Bethsaida to see what needs to be changed there, to see who needs to be carried down.

If we really care about freedom and peace, if we are really committed as Catholic educators to maintaining freedom and building the peace, then we must realize that the whole world is back at Bethsaida again. While Nicodemus questions whether or not he has the reason or the resources or the call or the courage or the information to begin again — to teach a better lesson, to free the new-found bound, to bring peace to minds at war — while Nicodemus rationalizes, the whole world is back at the healing pool at Bethsaida again, a whirling, bubbling, promising, but oppressive place.

In today's Bethsaida, the world is so close to being one and at the same time so deeply divided. Christianity is global but not different. Christian countries make as much war as peace; they build as many bombs as the countries and governments they label as killers. Christian businesses pay low wages for high priced goods. Christian engineers invent weapons to destroy the world. Christian governments cut the poor and the handicapped from the budget in order to cut the taxes of the rich.

Hope and despair walk hand in hand. The biological sciences make gain after gain in medicine while chemistry and physics plot death and destruction. Indigent peoples in one part of the world claim their independence while whole nations starve to death in another. Major nations fight puppet wars and small nations work to throw off oppression. The population of the world shifts to the Third World where over half the people are under 15. And hungry. A whole new world agenda is developing that is not being set by the wealthy nations of the West and the North. There is more stress now on human development, social needs, and the common good, and far less stress on old world powers, old values, and old centers of control.

And it is all happening at a dizzying pace. We are in the midst of the world's fastest total transformation. The biological development of humankind, from pre-hominid to homo-sapiens, took five million years .we are told. The social development of human society from tribes to structured societies took five thousand years. The technological development from agricultural society to industrialized society took five hundred years. But the movement from national sovereignty to a planetary interdependence linked by common social standards, technology, and economic networks has taken place in the last fifty years.

We live in a world of major social transformation. In such times two things happen: a sense of powerlessness or breakdown and a sense of possible breakthrough. Some are well fed and some die daily of hunger. Some have power and many are powerless. Half of all the people of the world — women — have little or no part in the decisions of government, military, economic, social, or ecclesial structures that affect them. Toxic waste and industry destroy whole regions of land and threaten the lives of children unborn. Satellites connect the world while Star Wars technology threatens to destroy it. Demographers tell us that there will be 2000 new cities by the year 2000, with 2000 new pockets of mass unemployment, 2000 new ghettoes created by the poor who rush to the cities for water and for bread, 2000 new places where the gap between the rich and poor widens daily. All of this will give rise to new world tensions and cube the pressures that militate against freedom and peace.

In a country where once we could teach children that wheat was our major export, we must now tell them that weapons are. A cursory review of world arms sales indicates that for all our talk about principles and allies, we have nevertheless armed our friends to fight our enemies — we armed South Vietnam to fight North Vietnam; our friends to fight our friends — we armed both Argentina and England; our enemies to fight our friends — we armed both Iran and Iraq; and our friends who then become our enemies — we armed Yemen, Cuba, Vietnam, and Nicaragua.

In a country that claims that its only role in the arms race is deterrence, it is we who have developed every weapons system first and we who have used them. In a country that can destroy the planet many times over, it is Christians who cannot sleep in peace until they know they can do it even more.

Oh, yes, we know and teach great breakthroughs in our time: scientific ability without political will. Global interaction without justice, though we know we are capable of human unity. Television, telephone lines, and transportation all show us that all of humankind has the same hopes, values, loves, and dreams. We all share a new world view, taken with a camera in outer space. And from that perspective comes a sense of phenomenal power as well as a sense of tragic powerlessness.

Are we as religious educators teaching anyone to speak to the problems of hunger? Are our schools teaching the land loss problems that come with erosion, population growth, and industrial abuse? Are we teaching in our schools that one half of the human species, women, has been disenfranchised? Are we teaching that air and water pollution, not a lack of scientific capacity, is destroying this planet? Are we teaching the technological dangers of toxic waste as well as we teach the technology itself? Are we facing our own global illiteracy and provincialism? Are we teaching that what harms the other will eventually harm us as well? Are we teaching the new-found demon of militarism? Are we teaching that we live in a world where multinational powers control trade and employment and profits without any system of international controls?

Indeed, Bethsaida is a familiar place. It's happening all around us. The waters stir today too for the wealthy, for the West, for white males. It's not true that the whole system is in chaos; some people are getting on, getting up, getting rich. But others wait their turn and are denied, while the rest of us, like Nicodemus, say nothing. That is this day's threat to freedom; that is this time's real obstacle to peace; that is this moment's call to Christian conscience.

Who will see the situation? Who will be born of the spirit and be willing to begin again? Who will be healed of their own sexism, racism, militarism and nationalism? Who will hold themselves accountable for the oppression of others? Who will do away with the process and politics of it all?

Who will hear the answer to begin again and to speak in the light as Jesus did? Not by saying, "Offer it up." Not by saying, "Let me hold you up." But by cutting through sexist, militarist, and nationalist systems saying "Get up" and then staying there to raise the poor and the powerless.

Do we want to know the reality and depth of our own teaching of the faith-life? Today ask a friend to tell you what three things you stand for and then ask what three things you have done to prove that.

Do you believe in the just distribution of resources? What have you done this year to prove it?

Do you stand for peace and nuclear disarmament? What three things have you done this year to prove it?

Do you stand for the gift of life and the equality of women in Church and society? Name one thing you have done this year that proves that.

Let there be no mistake. The point is not that everyone is guilty. The point is that everyone is responsible. The questions are important because this time it's our turn at Bethsaida. What we teach and how we teach it may well make a difference in a world that hasn't stood up straight in thirty-eight years.

Catechesis is not enough. Teachers are for times of peace. We need prophets now.

We live in a world where science, not industry, has become the great high priest of our time. The motto is no longer: "The greatest number of desirable goods for the maximum number of people at the cheapest possible cost." Now the motto of science is: "What can be done must be done and will be done, whether it ought to be done or not." Not the limits of the marketplace but only the limits of the mind will determine which products control our environment. The question is, "Who will teach freedom and peace to science?"

We live in a world where technology has not made the world smaller; technology has made the world one. War in the East stops production in the West. Scenes of famine in Africa appear on TV screens in American restaurants. Scenes of American two-and-three car garages appear on street corner TV's in Third-World villages. Decisions that make corporations in one country wealthy create an imbalance of employment and development in another. Who will teach freedom and peace to capitalism?

We live in a world where Christians have invented the high art of planetary cataclysm, where Christians argue "matchstick parity" and worry about who has the most matches in a situation where, since we are up to our necks in gasoline, only one match will do the job. We live in a world where the end of the world has been created by us and stored in the corn fields of Kansas. We have chosen to be Sparta rather than Athens. Who will teach freedom and peace to militarism run amok?

The answer depends on whether Catholic education succumbs to the caution of Nicodemus or is born again in our time to the courage and compassion of the Christ.

In our day, more than ever, we need religious education:

- that leads rather than certifies;

- that contributes to a just future rather than simply to an economically satisfying present;

- that is willing to question whether or not what is scientifically and economically possible is also humanly appropriate;

- that is built on curriculums of conscience, not just curriculums of content;

- that knows that peace is based on justice and bends itself to build it;

- that realizes that freedom is based on the sacrament of creation, and restructures itself to reflect the equality given by God.

The way is not easy. Nicodemus, remember, never returned again after he was told to begin over.

The obstacles to peace and freedom, just as their call, are deep within us. We must confront in ourselves the fear of polarization. "There are people in the parish who will not like this. They'll remove their children from the school." There are those who would preach prudence to the crucifix! We worry so much that some people will be upset that we are willing to let other people's human rights wait forever. On those days we have to remember that from the time of Peter and Paul the Church has known that tension does not have to divide; tension can also stretch and complete the body of Christ.

We must confront the institutionalism and complacency that can come with a hundred years of success. It is not enough for our institutions to be viable; they must also be prophetic. Simply doing better what others are doing well is not enough. Otherwise institutionalism will defeat us no matter how much we succeed. Our institutions must be Christian centers devoted to world peace, to equality, to social justice or none of them can be justified no matter how financially sound they are. As Nicodemus noted, courses in religion are no substitute for conviction.

We must confront and change the theology of domination. Sexism, racism, and militarism are of a piece, and sexism is their cornerstone. If we are committed to peace, our institutions will have to give more than theory to the freedom and equality of the sexes. Our textbooks will have to change as well as our language and our budgets.

Finally, we must confront the cancer of gringoism in the church. We have to teach the Peace Pastoral; we have to prepare students to make informed decisions about conscientious objection and selective conscientious objection; we have to confront and critique a false nationalism that apparently with ease destroys civilians, mines harbors in our own hemisphere and ties food to political money. We have to give the Russians a face and ask the right questions. The right question is not, "Who is for peace?" Who isn't for peace; who prefers war? No,the right question is, "How would Christ achieve peace, and so who can best achieve peace, those who make weapons or those who dismantle them?" There is no justification for submitting the human community to the threat of nuclear annihilation, the Peace Pastoral says. Not even nationalism, it seems.

The problem of Nicodemus and Bethsaida is clear. If we truly want Catholic education to make its contribution to freedom and peace in our day, we ourselves must first teach and live new role definitions. We ourselves must first live new standards of living. We ourselves must first live new military policy, foreign policy, and economic ideals. We must take our schools away from the secularism of professional preparation and return them to the challenge of the Gospel.

Nicodemus alerts us to what happens when we buy into a system. Jesus at Bethsaida shows us what can happen when we have the faith to change one. But do not be misled. There is a terrible cost.

They tell the story of a German woman during World War II who hid Jews. When her friends found out, they said, "Don't you realize that if you are discovered you yourself will be imprisoned, perhaps even executed?" The woman said clearly, "Yes, I know that." "Then why in heaven's name," they asked "are you doing it!" And she said simply: "Because the time is now and I am here."

This time is our time. This place is our place. We are the inheritors of a system bold with the heritage of freedom, burdened with the challenge of peace. Who will turn the Gospel into Good News in our time? If not us, who? If not now, when?

Remember, the paralytic didn't go to Bethsaida with faith; the paralytic knew that the waters moved every year. The paralytic didn't go to Bethsaida with love; the paralytic knew that God's gifts belonged also to him. The paralytic went to Bethsaida in the hope of finding a teacher whose faith was performative, a teacher who would carry him down.

May Paradise live in each of us, whatever we teach.

7. MARY WARD

From the age of fifteen Mary Ward believed she had a religious vocation but in seventeenth century England where to be a Catholic was to be an outlaw, her goal seemed an impossible one. Indeed, she made several false starts before she found her way: she first joined the Poor Clares in France as an extern Sister; after a year she left to establish a monastery of English Poor Clares, also in France, where she was taunted as a "runaway nun."

God had other plans for her. Back in England as a laywoman, she gathered seven other educated women around her and returned to France determined to establish a new kind of community which would combine religious life with the education of young girls. Her spiritual advisers were Jesuits for the most part.

After a serious illness, Mary Ward heard an inner voice that her new Institute should be established along Ignatian lines but adapted to a feminine way of life. When she submitted her proposal to Rome for approval in 1621, it contained several radical elements: it was to be a mixed life of contemplation and apostolic activity subject to the Pope alone, rather than to a male religious order and with no enclosure or habit.

Opposition from clergy and the Sacred Congregation in Rome eventually led to the suppression of the Institute in 1631. Mary Ward was taken as a prisoner to a convent of Poor Clares in Munich where she was

denied the support of both her friends and the sacraments. Only in 1877 was the vision of this valiant
woman vindicated when the Church gave full approval to her Institute.

In several of her letters to her community, Mary
Ward takes a position on women. The following essay
is based on those letters.

Mary Ward said, "I hope in God it will be seen that women in
time to come will do much."

The psalmist said, "How long, O God, will you cast us off? We
have no one to tell us, nor have we a prophet to say how long this
suffering will last."

For a woman of the twentieth century to read the life of seventeenth century Mary Ward is to know the depth of the psalmist's
lament. For women over the centuries, little has changed. The
forces arrayed against the participation of women in pastoral
ministry in Mary Ward's time resist women still. The ideas and
attitudes that branded women as inferior, as "but women," persist still. The proscriptions against the autonomy, independence
and equality of women which made Mary Ward's insights
heresy, which condemned this woman to ecclesiastical prison
and suppressed the religious group she founded, exist still. Certainly in some places today, as in Mary Ward's time, some
women enjoy a basically free environment. But nowhere are
women actually equal, either in church or society, and
everywhere male systems define, restrict and exclude women
from the inner sanctums where deals are cut and decisions are
made, even about them. Mary Ward, however, stands upright in
history to refute all of that. In the face of the greatest lie of life —
that women are inferior, inept, and incomplete both in nature
and in grace — Mary Ward brings "verity."

Mary Ward had convictions that confronted the given wisdom
of the age about the basic nature of women. One author calls the
ideas "dangerously novel for her time." The problem, unfortu-

nately, is that her ideas may be dangerously novel for our time as well. The important thing is that they demand consideration and give hope yet today.

Women and Grace

Mary Ward believed firmly that women were as capable of grace as men. Fervor, she argued despite the opposition of church men of the period, was a feminine strength as well as a male prerogative. But the implications of the position were ominous. If women were capable of finding God and maintaining their spiritual commitment without the guidance of a male, then the structures that mirrored the prevailing theology were endangered. The notion that spiritual perfection was possible for women struck at the roots of a system that not only pronounced women inherently weak but automatically put them under male spiritual directors, made them directly obedient to the chaplains and vicars and local Bishops into whose care and jurisdiction they were given, because, as one priest told Mary Ward, "women could not apprehend God."

Consequently, men wrote the constitutions of religious orders; men conducted the canonical visitation of convents; men directed the internal affairs of women's groups; only male members of an Order qualified to participate in the General Chapters or legislative assemblies of that Order. The spiritual immaturity of women was, in fact, the given upon which the entire system was based. To argue for the spiritual adulthood of women was to threaten the spiritual paternalism of the male church and to endorse the possibility of spiritual leadership in women, a concept that is only now coming into sharper focus as women have begun to do theology and to go to other women for spiritual direction and theological education.

Women as Bearers of the Faith

Mary Ward clearly believed that women were called to teach

the faith. Her argument is a compelling one even in our own day.
"If women were so inferior to men in all things," she reasons,
"why were they not exempted in all things as they are in some?"
Why, in other words, admit that they can do anything at all? If
women are naturally deficient in some things, naturally
excluded from some areas, are they not really inadequate in all?
Yet some things are required of them. She wrote: "Hath not God
appointed and commanded his apostles and others to preach.
God's words are not in vain. Besides, you know, there are par-
dons to any that in any sort shall teach or instruct. This is
granted to all, as well to women as to men." It is true that in the
seventeenth century Mary Ward did not question the submission of wives to husbands or the role of men in the sacramental
system or the "preaching of the faith in public churches," but she
simply calls "an error" the notion that women cannot conduct
their own spiritual lives or learn or teach. Inequity itself she un-
masked as proof of equality. Either women could do nothing and
so should be exempted from responsibility for anything; or
women were also able to give spiritual leadership and so should
be exempted from nothing. In our own time, the question of
exemption from some things but not from others, of having all of
responsibilities but only some of the rights of baptism, is becoming increasingly more evident and increasingly more serious. Women are said to be able to teach but not to preach; to pray
for others but not to bless them; to counsel sinners but not to for-
give them. If these insights of Mary Ward's are to continue to
be ignored, then the whole theology of baptism, Incarnation and
Eucharist must be rethought.

Women and Perfection

Mary Ward was intent on the fact that women could be perfect
as well as men. In fact, Mary Ward contested the notion that
men were by nature superior to women. "If we look upon men as
prophets, we shall see their imperfections, but if we look upon
them as men, we shall see them far otherwise. You may know

them by the fruits of their counsels," she instructed her Sisters. The teaching was a revolutionary one: men are not unusually graced creatures; they are human just as women are. Learn to discriminate in what they tell you and you will not be either misled or disillusioned. Obviously, when their counsels meant the derogation of women and the diminishment of the quality of their creation, there was in Mary Ward's mind no truth, no profit, no praise of God, no *veritas Domini* in that.

The tension, of course, lies in the fact that to this day the inference is that women cannot possibly be as perfect as men. Otherwise, how account for the fact that all the truths of the faith are discerned and defined by men only? How argue the fact that women are not permitted to teach in seminaries except by saying that no woman can possibly have anything to say to a man about God? How justify the notion that men can be ordained permanent deacons but women cannot when, as a matter of fact, women may, by special injunction at least, do everything of substance that deacons can do: distribute the Eucharist, baptize, preach, administer a parish? What is the continuing imperfection upon which this exclusion is based and how is it to be explained, especially in view of centuries of deaconesses in both the Eastern and the Western Church? In the words of Mary Ward: "It is certain God has looked upon you as he never looked upon any. Not better, not in a greater or more excellent manner, nor with more love, but as he never looked upon any." God, perhaps, but not men.

Women, Faith and Feminism

Mary Ward saw commitment to feminism as a sanctifying concept and an eternal truth. Convinced that her insights about women were from God, she accepted as her spiritual duty the moral obligation to proclaim them, despite almost fanatical opposition from those clerics and cardinals alike who considered nuns without cloister, choir, habits, and direct male control as heretics. In several speeches to her Sisters she repeats insistently her disagreement with the Father Minister who insisted that women could not maintain the fervor of their religious commitment without men. "With respect to the good Father, I must still say that it is not truth but a lie to say that fervor must necessarily decay, and that we are 'but women.' He may have much knowledge, and perhaps he hath all other knowledge and I have only this knowledge and the light of this only verity, by which perhaps, I must be saved."

For Mary Ward in the seventeenth century and for many Christian feminists in the twentieth, it is the Gospel itself that compels that sexism must be confronted wherever it is if the Church is to be credible. Insight into the truths of God was the essence of "verity" to Mary Ward. Much in the temper of evangelist Mary Dyer years later who said, "Truth is my authority; not authority my truth," Mary Ward pressed beyond the conventions of the system to the center of the vision.

Women, Faith and Dependence

Mary Ward made distinctions about dependence that tap both the best and worst of Catholic theology. Either women, too, have consciences and must follow them or they do not and therefore cannot be bound to them. Mary Ward, in other words, wanted women to be dependent but she did not want dependent women. She wanted women whose dependence was on God and who therefore were empowered by "verity," not made powerless in the name of God. Independence, she felt, was essential for women. In a case study of a convent that failed, she blames the failure not on the fact that the women lost contact with the Fathers of the Society or because they were women, but "because they placed their affections more in the esteem of those men that for the present guided them than in this verity which is only God." The point is, of course, that the women went astray because they never took charge of their own lives in the first place; that they made the men who were over them their gods; that they had given their consciences away.

What is more, she understood that true dependence differed from control. "I beseech you all," she wrote, "for God's love, to love verity and true dependence and not to adhere to the Superior, to this Father or this creature for affection, so that if they are lost, all is lost." Her concept is a dangerous one. It leads to decision-making; it leads to personal responsibility; it precludes blind obedience; it makes God the ultimate norm of every action and puts women in charge of their own actions. It is the kind of philosophy of creation that shakes the foundations of hierarchical systems. And it was not accepted; neither then in Mary Ward nor now in the new forms of government that have emerged in religious life for women since Vatican II. Women believe that Mary Ward was right, that the rights and responsibilities of women must be recognized and accepted if the church is ever to be a whole church. She wrote with bold clarity: "Heretofore we have been told by men we must believe (and) it is true we must. But, let us be wise and know what we are to believe and what not, and not to be made to think we can do nothing."

Self-Definition

Of all of her perceptions, the keenest may be Mary Ward's awareness of the effect of male definitions of womanhood on the development of women. She simply tells her Sisters to pay no attention to them: "You may know them by the fruits of their counsels. For what can this profit you, to tell you that you are but women, weak and able to do nothing, and that fervor (commitment? stability? spiritual development?) will decay."

The problem is not a small one. That the definition of women by men is limiting and false is difficult enough. The effects of these very definitions on the development of women are even worse. If psychology has taught us nothing else, it is at least clear now that the oppressed internalize the message of the oppressor; that people live down to their stunted expectations. Inferiority, in other words, is learned from the standard setters of a society whose access to the schools and courts and legislatures of a people have the power to define the rights of others. It is precisely about the nature and possibilities of women that women must educate the church, or humanity may never come to know the fullness of God's creation. If women had no other ministry than this, the world and the church would be different tomorrow.

Women and Self-Development

Mary Ward loved both learning and knowledge, but learning, she knew, could corrupt knowledge. There were, as a matter of fact, things for women to unlearn. And that could be done only by knowledge. "The verity of our Lord not the verity of men, nor the verity of women." It was ultimate truth that Mary Ward sought for her Sisters and instructed them to seek. Women may be perfect as well as men, she argued, "if they love verity and seek true knowledge." It was lack of "true knowledge" that made actions which otherwise looked good "to be unseemly." Mary Ward asks women to look beyond the mind of men into the mind of God. Mary Ward was asking for speculation and contemplation and reason of the highest degree from women. She expected it. "I entreat you to love and seek truth and the knowledge it brings you unto, for the end which it brings you unto is God. It is want of knowledge or want of true consideration of God which is the end of knowledge that we fear, not the words of greatness, not of princes or any other things besides God." Mary Ward asks women to be all they can be regardless of who says they cannot. And Mary Ward paid the price of her knowledge of God's creating will for women as do women today who seek to direct their lives and contact their God without male control or male consecration.

Women and the Development of Ministry

Mary Ward gave her life to the development of this new lifestyle and service of women. It was "knowledge and verity" which impelled her. She knew, however, that real reasons are not always acceptable reasons for doing something and cautioned her Sisters that their love of their company or institute would be the very thing that would lead them to lie, to give one reason or explanation or defense of a thing when you really knew it was another. "To bring others to know truth, you must lie. I mean you must say that which is not verity and that which you know is not truth because if you speak truth to them, they will not understand it. Verily, it is a pitiful thing that to bring others to truth, we must speak that which is not verity, and which we know is not truth."

The circumstance continues. Whatever women do must look like an accident rather than a call, an expectation, a birthright. Women are given parishes to administer because "there is no one else to do it." Women are given the Eucharist to carry "because there is no one else to carry it." Women are given pastoral programs to direct "because no one else is qualified." But women are given none of these things for the real reason: they are baptized; they are committed; they are human; they have been given gifts by God that must be used in the name of God.

Women and Spiritual Leadership

Mary Ward understood her opposition well. She knew that men considered them radicals, "new beginners of a course never thought of before." She knew that the expectation was that they would fail and not be able to "bring to pass things beyond the compass of such weak creatures as they have ever esteemed women to be, who expect to see our fervor decay and all come to nothing, ourselves to shame and confusion." But she knew too that there were others who looked upon them "with another conceit, expecting all the world to be bettered by us."

And through it all she persisted. Through the local investigations and complaints, through the accusations and disapproval, through the examination by the College of Cardinals, through the suppression of the Order, through the house-arrest in the convent in Angers. So strong was her faith that women, too, were created in the image of God and that women were no lesser creatures than men that she laid down her own life to release the lives and gifts of other women.

But in 1986, though some gains have definitely been made for some women — in education, in legal rights, in social inclusion, in theological developments and pastoral participation — nevertheless most of the poor, most of the hungry, most of the disenfranchised of the world are still women. All of the authorities of the Church are still men and the laws still prescribe cloisters, choirs, habits, and male approval for women's religious groups. Women are still considered inadequate to contact God sacramentally. In 1986 Mary Ward still speaks to us all about how to minister to our own times.

Women must know their own worth and instill that worth in other women, Mary Ward instructs. Women must seek and speak eternal truth regardless of the lesser truths that bind. Women must develop their own spirituality, independently of male mentors, and hold fast to it because other spiritualities are derogations of women. Women must claim equality in the face of inequity. Women must be "truly dependent" and so independent of everything that is not of God. Women must see themselves as entrusted with the Gospel and preach it. Women must listen to women. Women must see commitment to the full development of women as a moral and therefore a sanctifying obligation. Women must be steadfast in their commitment. Women must not fear to speak their truth to the great and the princely "to effect or bring to pass whatever is necessary." Indeed, she taught, women had special gifts to bring to ministry and men were not infallible in regard to the development of women.

Mary Ward's sense of woman was a searing truth in the heart of the Church and in the hearts of the women as well who persisted over time in the ideals of this prophet. So certain was she of the truth of her being that her most poignant insight into the power of creation within her may well be her declaration: "I confess that if there were not God, or if I did not do what I do for Him, that which I find within myself were sufficient to make me do all I do or shall do. And indeed in that I am unsatisfied because I know not from wherever this proceeds, though I hope, well."

Mary Ward did not prevail, except in part. A theology of limitation is the catechism on women to this day. But Mary Ward does raise both questions and models that will not die. Does God value women as much as Mary Ward did? And if so, why does not the male Church?

The answer given to women about the strictures on their gifts when all other answers — intellectual, biological, and social — have been given the lie, has always been "tradition." But the real issue for our time is, is this the tradition? Is the exclusion of women from the administrative and sacramental life of the Church because this was not supposed to be or because no one would allow it to be? Is not the continual re-emergence of great women who do great things that great men say may not be done by women also part of the tradition? The question is, why do we never legitimate that part of the tradition? Mary Ward already had the answer. She wrote: "I would to God that all men understood this verity, that women, if they will, may be perfect and if they would not make us believe we can do nothing and that we are but women, we might do great matters."

It is 400 years later. The spiritual leadership of women depends yet on the witness, the verity, of courageous women. It depends as well on the honesty of conscientious men who will call their own systems to the Gospel truth. Or as a contemporary feminist said, "If you don't risk anything, you risk even more."

8. THE ORDINATION OF WOMEN: A QUESTION OF AUTHORITY OR THEOLOGY

Perhaps the most insightful statement on the question of the ordination of women in the Roman Catholic Church which has emerged in stark terms in the church in the United States comes from a dialogue between an American woman and a local bishop. "I have a grave theological problem with the question of the ordination of women," the bishop said to the woman. "I want you to realize that you and I have a fundamental difference on that issue," he went on, "but I also want you to know that if the Church gave permission for the ordination of women, I would ordain a woman immediately." And the woman said, "In other words, Bishop, you don't really have a theological problem with the question at all. You have an authority problem that is masking as a theological one."

The conversation may well be a microcosm of the ordination problem. In the United States women continue to prepare for the ordained ministry, if not in Catholic seminaries then in ecumenical consortiums or in Protestant seminaries. Those who are not in formal theological training press for insertion into the pastoral system of the parishes. Some have left the Church altogether to participate in women's liturgies and faith development. What is the basis for all of this? What kind of women are these? What are the implications of this for the Church? Where is this movement going?

Basis of the Problem

The Woman's Ordination Conference, founded in 1975 with a national convention of over 1000 women, lay and religious, made the question of the ordination of women a public and institutionalized question. One year later, the Vatican document, "The Declaration on the Question of the Admission of Women to the Ministerial Priesthood," purported to put an end to the movement but, in fact, only heightened the question. The document made two major claims for the exclusion of women from priesthood in the Catholic Church: first, that Jesus was male and so men are clearer images of Christ, and secondly, that the tradition of the Church prohibited the admission of women to ordained ministry.

Advocates of women's ordination, on the other hand — theologians, scripture scholars, and Christians concerned that both the nature and the future of the Church are bound up in the question of the role of women — responded with arguments, questions, and analyses which are sure to keep the question alive. Maleness and tradition, they argued, were inadequate foundations for the sacrament of Orders in the light of other weightier considerations.

Proponents or students of the question of the ordination of women cite four basic issues which they say reduces ordination to a matter of church discipline and authority rather than to revealed truth.

In the first place, proponents argue, the exclusion of women from priesthood undermines the credibility and effectiveness of other sacraments or doctrines of the Church. The efficacy of baptism, grace, and the Incarnation are all brought into question, they propose, if somehow the meaning of these differs between men and women. Either baptism does erase differences — "Jew and Greek, slave and free, male and female" (Gal. 3:18) — or it does not. Either all grace is given freely to both males and

females, or women are lesser creatures capable of less blessing
and gift, in which case the nature of creation and the nature of
the human race are both diminished. Either Christ came so that
all would have fullness of life and have it more abundantly or
the Incarnation is more the salvation of males than it is of the
human race.

That Jesus is male, this group reasons, is incidental to the fact
that Jesus became flesh, and so identical to the human race and
like us all.

In the final analysis, it is the model of Jesus to which both
groups point to rest their case. Opponents of the ordination of
women point to the fact that Jesus did not "ordain" a woman,
that no women were at the Last Supper during the institution of
the Eucharist and do not therefore qualify for priestly ordination.

Proponents, on the other hand, draw from Jesus' associations
with women to make the case that Jesus did accept women, contrary to the cultural norms of the time, and involved them in the
priestly ministry of proclamation with Him: a woman bore
Jesus; a woman announced Jesus to the Samaritans and a
woman announced Jesus' Resurrection to "Peter, John and the
others;" the rabbi Jesus taught women; Jesus recognized
women in public contrary to his contemporaries and raised
them from the dead as of equal value to men. That women were
not at the Last Supper, this group maintains, is no argument
against the ordination of women, unless you are also willing to
argue that women should not receive the Eucharist on the same
basis. Here apparently someone made a decision to include
women despite the Last Supper model; why not for ordination
also?

Centuries of tradition itself, however, are to many minds an
imposing argument in itself. Others, on the other hand, take the
position that the tradition prohibiting the ordination of women
is less a matter of sacrament and more a matter of the cultural

norms and social structures long common to other facets of society as well but now changing. The fact that slavery existed for almost 2000 years and was defended theologically, they point out, is no justification for its continuance.

Obviously, the historical-theological differences in viewpoint are likely to persist for a considerable amount of time. There is, at the same time, a distinct but related question. What kind of women are these who seek ordination? Are they mentally well-balanced? What are their motives? Are both their personalities and their aims compatible with priesthood?

An in-depth psychological investigation of a random sampling of women who feel called to priesthood in the Catholic Church, *Called to Break Bread?,* concerned itself with psychological adaptation and comparative analyses of similar data from the 1972 National Opinion Research Center study of "The Catholic Priest in the United States: Sociological Investigations." The findings revealed that a large proportion of women seeking ordination (77-96 percent) had well-integrated personalities and were potentially effective ministers. In terms of personality development, in fact, the women showed considerably more development than the ordained priests studied, particularly in the area of interpersonal relations. Most (72 percent) were women religious whose pastoral involvements and experience were already tried. Over half of the women were of Irish and German descent. Most were highly educated, many in theology, scripture studies, and religious education. Almost three-quarters of the group held master's degrees; another ten percent held either bachelor degrees or earned doctorates. Over half were already working in positions of church administration or staffing church facilities. Of most interest, perhaps, is the fact that neither a desire for power nor a singular commitment to feminism as a distinct philosophy marked either their expressed motives or psychological profiles. The women spoke of the need to respond to the call of God within them, to service, and to the full development of the Church.

Whatever the theological debate, another reality impinges as well. According to statistics released by the Vatican and confirmed by public sources, the majority of the Catholics of the world are routinely deprived of the sacraments. Women as a class, in religious orders for instance, are denied the sacraments unless men can be found to provide the service. Sixty percent of the Catholics of the world live in Third World countries, but more than seventy percent of the priests serve the churches of the West where their numbers are declining. In some places, the ratio of priests to lay Catholics has dropped as low as 5 to 10,000.

The sacramentality of the Church and the style of Christian ministry is obviously in flux, and the whole question of whether the Church is to prefer maleness to Eucharist may well become the central Church issue of the century. In the meantime, in a 1978 national study of Benedictine Sisters in the United States, two-thirds of whom were over 60 years of age, almost nine out of ten completely rejected the thesis that men are clearer images of God than women are. Over half thought that women should be included on all decision-making bodies in the Church — national, diocesan, and curial. Almost two-thirds felt that they have an obligation to support the ordination of women.

The ordination of women is far more than an academic debate, however justified, and for that reason alone is bound not to go away. Whether the bishop or the woman, authority or theology, prevails remains to be seen. What is clear is that every day both the theological and the social context of the discussion is changing.

9. DIVINELY ORDAINED? RELIGIOUS CREATION MYTHS AND THE RELATION OF MILITARISM TO SEXISM

The Preamble to the Constitution of UNESCO states quite clearly: War begins in the minds of human beings. Since this is so, the minds of human beings must also be capable of ending war. It is time for the Peace Movement to concentrate on the causes as well as the effects of violence. It is time to trace them to their source, to run them down, to flush them out, to expose the roots of a vast network of oppression and disdain for the lives of others. It is time to change people's minds about the morality of war.

Unfortunately, the root of the problem may lie in religion's theology of woman.

The condition of women in society is an uninterrupted history of diminished development. What's worse, this oppression of women has been not only historical but universal. In every culture, in every time, violence against women has been constant and normative and sophisticated. And it has taken every form — physical, social, and psychological.

Women were the first slaves. An early hieroglyph for "slave," for instance, was the symbol "woman held in hand." Women slaves, of course, were easier to capture and keep than men would be, more useful in the domestic arena, an instrument for the perpetuation of the male line, and a symbol of success, a kind of primitive example of conspicuous consumption.

Not only were women the first slaves, however. They have also been the majority of slaves throughout history. The only exception to this social truth, in fact, lies in the slave system of North America and the Caribbean, where slavery became essential to the industrial organization of the time. Nieboer, in fact, in his now classic and definitive work, *Slavery as an Industrial System,* completely excluded women from the study on the grounds that "slavery proper does not exist where there are none but female slaves." The subjection of women, in other words, was a condition that was essential — of the essence of women — widespread, natural, and to be taken for granted. Women as a class have, as well, been historically deprived of the education that would enable them to sustain themselves, to lead others, and to decide their own fates. The university system of the thirteenth century, designed to prepare the leaders of the Western World in the classical reservoir of learning of the time, was simply closed to women, despite the fact that some of the best monastery schools of Europe had until that time been run by nuns. With the exclusion of women from the universities, however, women soon lost contact with the educational stream of the times, and so their schools lost credibility and effectiveness. By the seventeenth century the popular dictum prescribed that "women need enough geography to find their way around the house and enough chemistry to keep the pot boiling." Woman had become a completely domesticated animal with her highest function the service of others.

In nineteenth century United States, young women were allowed to go to school in the summers only, when boys would be in the fields for the harvest and so not in need of the seats and the attention. Even then, the curriculum for girls contained only writing, drawing, embroidery, music, dancing, and religious readings, subjects designed to make them good mothers and wives, not necessarily full human beings. Not until 1850 in the United States did the first independent secular college allow women to matriculate for a college degree, and then only on condition that they wash the clothes, clean the rooms, and serve the meals of the male students. Until after the Second World War, law and medical schools either refused admission to women entirely or set quotas of no more than 5 percent. Today, still, two-thirds of the illiterate of the world are women.

Pornography, prostitution, rape, and wife-beating remain male pastimes in a male society. It is not true that prostitution is the oldest profession. The fact is that it is the only profession allowed to many women in many societies because it serves the male population without threatening it. Pornography is a four billion dollar industry in the United States alone. Rape victims are battered by the courts as well as by the attacker, and wife-beating is winked at by the system. Women, in other words, uneducated and underdeveloped, have become the playthings and the property of the world.

The justification, of course, was the "unity of the spouses." Since there was only one person in marriage, the woman's legal existence was suspended. Bacon argued, for instance, that men are given "power and dominion over women to keep her by force, if necessary, within the bound of duty."

In the United States, the laws governing women became the model for the creation of laws to govern slaves.

Today, according to Straus and Gelles in the work *Behind Closed Doors,* two million women are beaten in the United States yearly. In two-thirds of all marriages, the woman is beaten at least once. Twenty-five percent of all married women are beaten weekly. Twenty percent of the emergency medical services provided to women in American hospitals follow wife-beatings. Twenty-five percent of all female suicide attempts are by beaten women. One out of every four female murder victims is killed by her husband or her boyfriend. Women, researchers tell us, are beaten every eighteen seconds and raped every three minutes.

Violence against women does not happen sometimes. Violence against women happens always.

On the backs of women, too, the poverty of the world falls hardest. Employment is no cure for it, for women are confined to areas of low pay and are paid less than men with less education, even less than men who do exactly the same work.

Women are psychologically diminished by underdevelopment, trivialization, invisibility, and the self-hate that comes from oppression. They have few rights in law; they are removed from the language; they are denied leadership. Women hold only 10 percent of the leadership positions in government, only 5 percent of the executive positions in business and no percent at all of the official positions of the Church.

The question is why? How can we account for the continual and violent oppression and suppression of women as a class? What meaning does that have for society at large? What meaning does that have for the Peace Movement? What meaning does that have for the Church?

The answer, it seems, must lie in the religious doctrine of female inferiority. Somewhere, somehow men got the idea that their control of women was not only acceptable but actually necessary and defensible and right. Religion has always provided that rationale.

Religion is simultaneously mystery and meaning. Religion asks the great questions of life and purports to know their answers. Why do we exist? Where did we come from? How did life begin? What is God like? What does God expect of us? These are issues to which the other institutions of society relate. On the answers to these questions depend both the ethics of our interpersonal relationships and the nature of our institutions.

The answers that religion brings to the great mysteries of life become the foundations of ethics and the basis of human organization. Religion says who we are and what our relationship to one another must be. What religion says, in other words, about the fundamental human assemblage becomes the glue of human

institutions, the basis of ethical principles, and the source of social practice. The problem is that religion's name for woman is
negative. The problem is that this diminishment of half the
human race validates and legitimates multiple other forms of
violence as well.

What is important to remember, however, is that religions
must warp their own fundamental revelation to do it.

Every major religion provides two dimensions on life: first, it
explains the origin of life, and second, it interprets the meaning
of life. The first dimension, the Creative Principle, explains as
revealed truth the nature of the beginning, the source, the nature of human life. The second dimension of religious truth, the
Creation Myths, describes the relationship of God to people, of
people to God, of people to people. The interpretation of the creation myths, consequently, is crucial to the development of society. And it is precisely these interpretations which are the basis
of sexism and, by implication, of militarism.

The basic problem lies in the fact that in every major world
religion the feminine is revealed as a co-equal part of the creative principle, either as pure spirit, as hermaphroditic being, or
as one of a co-equal divine couple. Yet in every major world religion women are interpreted in the religious writings of men as
inherently blighted, inferior, or dangerous to males and so to be
controlled and feared. The theology of domination that derives
from such a warped view of life has easy application to any group
of others who are seen as threat to the system in control. And
every major world religion reflects this tension between the
basic equality of human nature and the need to control it.

Hinduism

Early Hinduism, with its recognition of Brahman as the Universal self, the impersonal absolute, the One, saw boundless fertility as proof of the existence of a great mother goddess who
peopled the earth. With the fact that from Mother Earth, how-

ever, came both good and bad, spirit and matter, blessing and danger, came also the need for explanation and understanding. The Shiva-Kali myth did just that. The goddess Kali, asked to save her people, is successful and breaks into an ecstatic dance of joy which raises the fear that her undisciplined emotion will shake and break the foundations of the earth. To save the people from the danger of Kali herself, her husband Shiva throws her to the ground and restrains her. The interpretation given to Hindu women was a simple one: Just as female fertility had to be constrained by Father Heaven whose spirit would fertilize the earth and bring order to the undisciplined feminine principle, so the social order demanded that husbands control their wives. With this explanation, the dualism of matter and spirit was firmly in place in Indian society and social restrictions on women became both inevitable and necessary. In early Vedic society, consequently, women had a certain amount of freedom and status which emanated from a respect for the female power to give life, but they were expected to be dependent, docile wives whose husbands, like Father Heaven, were ordained to control them and their errant activities. The social effects of the enculturating myth went deep. Women had status in Hindu society because obviously women had power over life. But good women were to be subservient to men as dependent and docile wives. By the fifth century B.C.E. the marriage age of females had dropped to the age of five. Education and independence were lost. The salvation of a woman depended on her rebirth as a man in reward for having been a good (docile) wife who bore male children. Even after death, a man controlled his wife: she could not remarry and she was to do penance for his death. Widowhood and with it destitution was the woman's lot for having caused her husband's death by virtue of her own bad *karma*. *Suttee*, the practice of women's being allowed to throw themselves on the funeral pyre of the husband if their love for him had been perfect, became preferable to a life of poverty and abandonment.

Woman was, in effect, the creator of evil in the world. Whatever her power, however great her energy, she was obviously responsible for what came into the world and the disorder, disturbance and the downfall of social order that came with it. Women were seen as the source of the world's trouble, the birthers of the material. And the deduction that followed was debilitating: If women were responsible for matter, then men were the carriers of the spiritual or higher life. The interpretation of the myth became a weapon against an entire class of people and the social effects are with us still.

Buddhism

The Buddha, concerned with discovering the way to the fullness of life rather than with dealing with its origin took the position that *nirvana* — enlightenment and desirelessness — was possible to both women and men. That revelation, of course, should have guaranteed to women the education, authority, property, management, and the interpretation of the mysteries of the faith after the time of Buddha as it did during his life. The interpretation of the myth of the Demon Mara, however, was used eventually to justify the suppression of women. The story reads that the daughters of the Demon Mara — Desire, Pleasure and Passion — were arrayed against Buddha to test his Desirelessness. Though Buddha prevailed, the message is clear. Women are an obstacle to the achievement by men of a full spiritual life. When celibacy is institutionalized as the highest state of desirelessness after the Buddha, women are seen as an enemy of monkish perfection and must be shunned. True, Buddhist religious life, the Sangha, offered an alternative beyond marriage and motherhood that Indian women had not enjoyed in the past. Nevertheless, the institutionalization of male celibacy as the perfect manifestation of a desireless state, the continuing image of women's insatiable sexual needs, and the merger over time of Buddhism with Hinduism led to their fettering in other ways.

Women, as a result, are permitted to participate in Buddhist religious life, but only in obedience to monks. Women can be abandoned at any time to enable men to pursue enlightenment. Women are seen as having bad karma. Women are made dependent for life on the control and direction of men. Hinduism, which sees women as responsible for the creation of matter and its dangers, is now overlaid with Buddhism which sees women as responsible for spiritual entrapment and in need of structures that oppress. The stage is set, then, for systems that claim to be equal, look equal, and profess equality but which cling to patterns that justify the oppression of women in the name of salvation.

Only in popular Indian devotions — Mahayana Buddhism and Hindu bhakti or tantrism — was dualism suspect, wisdom feminine, and all things said to be capable of triggering enlightenment. In these faiths androgyny became the major religious symbol. Some depictions of divinity, in fact, were half male and half female beings in which the soft and the strong, the beautiful and the powerful dimensions of life were joined. Unfortunately, these cultic diversions were short-lived in the face of the older, longer traditions and without much social influence in the face of ancient beliefs. To this day, and despite civil legislation to the contrary, dowries are still paid in India; marriages are still arranged; a woman's salvation still depends on docile subservience to a husband; women may still be abandoned for the sake of the man's spiritual enlightenment; women still have inferior religious status; daughters are still bad karma; and the life of a woman still depends on the gratuitous kindness of a man.

Confucianism

In China Confucianism, the codification of Buddhist principles to bring harmony to society through filial piety, goodness, and social propriety, simply accepted the notion of female inferiority and corruption and set about to institutionalize it. Women, the religious thought continued, were by nature simply inferior beings whose undisciplined natures polluted attempts to contact the divine and would be punished after death (as tradition maintained) for having produced this pollution. Female infanticide, concubinage, girl sales, and footbinding became the natural outcome of a society unabashedly based on notions of hierarchy and domination. In fact, the common term for "girl" translated "slave girl" as well. Women existed only for the procreation necessary to maintain the ancestor worship that had become the logical continuation of the principle of the oneness of life. Women themselves, however, could offer no ancestor worship since tradition dictated that the feminine nature was a fundamentally corrupt one.

Confucianism was the state religion of China from 57 BCE to 1911 CE. On the prescriptions and protocol of Confucianism rested the social patterns of the Far East for centuries. For Confucius, the Tao, or Way of God, was hierarchy, order, and ethics. In that hierarchy, women were subject to men and inheritors of social controls designed to assure their fidelity. In this way, family stability and the orderly continuance of the lineage so important to ancestor worship became the burdensome obligation of the woman. "The Will of Heaven," Confucius argued, "begins in the relation between man and woman and ends in the vast reaches of the universe." The natural law theme was clear and commanding and woman's responsibility for the peace and order of the family was attributed to the mind of God.

Taoism

Taoism (604 BCE) softened the situation somewhat. Human nature, Lao Tzu the Master said, was an admixture of yin and yang energies that could be balanced through meditation and nonviolence. Tao, the way of nature, was gentle, "worthy to be the Mother of all things." The cardinal virutes of Taoism were humility and resignation rather than Confucian action and achievement. The power gained by practicing Tao was symbolized by water, valley, infant, and female. Yin was not subservient to yang as tradition had it, the Taoist claimed, but correlative and indispensable for the balance and wholeness of nature. There was to be no female infanticide in Tao. But Taoism was overshadowed by both Confucianism and Buddhism and in its ascendancy gained only one cultural consequence of note, the legal eradication of female infanticide.

The social profile is a clear one: In the face of a warring society and social upheaval, authoritarianism prevailed in China and with it the creation myth of domination rather than equality. Concubinage, female infanticide, the sale of girls, and footbinding, the height of Confucian misogyny, lasted until the twentieth century. Order, it seems, is the need to assure power to the powerful and to equate those with force with the force of God.

Shintoism

In Japan, women fared well for a time. The native religion, Shintoism, took as its Creative Principle the concept of the Divine Primal Couple whose Sun Goddess created the Japanese Islands. Women, as a result, had both religious and social import in early Japanese society. Shamanesses, female religious figures, could become channels for the spirits, the kami, and so women gained a modicum of social and cultural importance for a limited time. But the Japanese, in their respect for Chinese culture, eventually adopted Confucian ethics and, in turn, its depreciation of women. By the twelfth century, Confucian ethics and the misogyny that derived from it were refined to high art by the Samurai, the militaristic feudalism that became Japan's ideal society by the twelfth century. "Harmony" became the control by rational men over the demonic power of women. Under the Samurai, women lost civil rights, political power, and education. Now, instead, a young girl was instructed in the obligation to suicide if her chastity was violated, if her husband was in danger, or if her relationship with her husband threatened his loyalty to his Lord. Bushido, this unwritten code of disciplined loyalty to the master, touched women's lives in every aspect.

Women were used for pleasure; wives for the management of the home. Both existed as second-class citizens in a world that purported to bring harmony to a universe where rational men were intended to dominate the demonic power of women.

Western Civilization

But a religion of fertility goddesses is one thing, monotheism another. How account for sexism and its relation to militarism in a Christian culture that claims a God of pure spirit who replies to the question, "What is your name?" with the answer, "I am who am." Where is the inferiority construct in that and what needs to be questioned there? What can possibly be the association between sexism and militarism in a world view that claims that everything that such a God made is good?

In Western civilization two religious world views predominate, one the root of the other. Judaism and Christianity claim a common vision of human creation: the God of Being created all things and people "in God's own image" as male and female and for their eternal happiness. Their sin led to their banishment from paradise and to their punishment, he to earn bread by the sweat of his brow and she to bear children in pain.

In both religious traditions women are said to be honored, but the stage is small and the lines totally biological. Long gone is the commitment to a creation made in "the image of God," an implicit admission of the feminine as well as the masculine element in the creative source. Rather, women came quickly to be described as the after-thought of human life and the source of its trouble — the one made for the other, second and therefore secondary, inferior instead of identical and equal to the other as "bone of my bone," and "just like me." Adam, the first man, says in the Judeo-Christian scriptures, "The woman you gave me, she caused me to sin." Her seduction, not his equally bad judgment or co-conspiracy, was defined by male exegetes as the cause of humankind's loss of primitive grace, and so responsibility came to fall harshest on the woman. The social structures of each society reflect the ideology of male rationality and female immorality and decrepitude to this day.

Judaism

Judaism defines marriage as a prime symbol for God's relationship with the people of Israel and the good wife as one who bore male children. Unfortunately, what made a woman valuable also made her unclean and therefore a spiritual threat to Jewish men on whom all major religious responsibility devolved. Women were segregated, dependent, and limited. They did not have the right to full religious participation, public intervention, or authority. What is more, inferior by nature and a temptress, a woman lost the right to the autonomy of full personhood because of Eve's sin.

Christianity

In Christianity Jesus' acceptance of women, his balance of images, his teaching, his even-handed expectations were soon overlaid with rabbinic morality and a preference for Genesis II, the creation story of an earlier date that curses Eve to subordination. Just as the Jews had struggled to define themselves against the Caananites whose religious practices included women, the early Christian communities trod a line between Judaism and gnosticism. With vowed celibacy in the third century came the dread of women and the need to control them. Augustine argued that woman was no full image of God unless joined to a man who was her head. By the thirteenth century, Thomas Aquinas, working from Aristotle and Augustine, had defined woman as weaker in substance than men, defiled in intellect and in moral character, sexually promiscuous, and without spiritual strength (Aquinas 466; 472). God was exclusively "Father" not YHWH. Now God was male, though pure spirit. In this cosmology, males are, of course, closer to God. Everything else follows logically; the dictum marks Western culture to this day.

On the basis of this world view, Western women have taken a vow of obedience to men, been denied full spiritual participation by their churches, been defined by their biology. Their abilities are limited, their purpose sexual, their function domestic.

Islam

In seventh century Arabia, Islam brought to life the same creation myth and religious history that Jewish monotheism had already described. Mohammed did not preach a new religion; he simply preached a new prophecy of the religion that was endemic to the area. In his telling, as in Genesis I and in Jesus, women enjoyed a fundamental religious equality with men. Mohammed outlined, too, the social effects of that philosophy in ways uncommon to the area: a woman was allowed consent to marriage; polygamy was limited; divorce was regulated; she had property rights and in Mohammed's time was even permitted to pray in the mosques. But whatever gains accrued to women were quickly eroded by the last line of the Koran itself: "Men are in charge of women because Allah hath made one of them to excel the other, and because they spend their property (for women's support). Good women are obedient." On the basis of this dictum, later ages enforced veiling and *purdah* — seclusion and harems for women — to avoid the sexual danger presented by women, whose entire bodies were considered sexual and unfit for either mosque or marketplace. The move rendered women socially marginal and socially incompetent. The husband's control was absolute. She could be imprisoned, even killed, for disobedience and divorced both without cause and without cult. All the man had to say was "I divorce you" and the woman was condemned to poverty and disgrace. To this day, over seventy four million cliterodectomies are performed in continental Africa alone. This established practice remains to as-

sure against infidelity and to release women from what is said
to be their insatiable bondage to sex (Hosken 3).

Social Intersections and Effects

It is clear, then, that whatever its motive and whatever its
source, religion as inherited by us validates violence against
women. Creation stories are used to prove that some humans
are more human than other humans. Whether creation is
explained as the result of Mother Earth, the intercourse of a
primeval couple, or the creative act of an integrated male/
female being, the fall of man (sic) is attributed to the disordered
appetite or polluting chemistry of woman. It is religion, in other
words, that teaches that inequality was built into the human
race, that some people are by nature closer to God than other
people, that some people are innately more virtuous than other
people, that some people are made for other people's use, that
some people have both the right and the duty to control other
people, and that these people know who they are.

The corruption of the creation myths of each major religion of
the world, including Christianity, has been used by men to assure the ascendancy of men. Men were entitled to women as part
of their birthright. Whether the women in question agreed or
not, men took as divine decree the right to buy them, collect
them, trade them, and fight over them. Religion, in other words,
in its derogation of half the human race, has created a theology
of domination that despite all spiritual maxims to the contrary,
makes generalized violence, aggression, and international
militarism not just logical but necessary in order to control what
must be administered by men who have been "given dominion."

The natural inequality of women has been institutionalized
by the woman's marriage vow of obedience and used to justify
both discrimination and abuse. Wife beating was specifically allowed by canon law (Power 35) and enshrined in civil law as well
which sanctioned the right of "reasonable chastisement" (Bauer

and Ritt 103). The great English barrister Blackstone, in his law treatises of the 1760s, reaffirmed medieval law's approval of "moderate correction," noting that since the husband was responsible for his wife's misbehavior, the law had entrusted to him the power of "restraining her by domestic chastisement" (103).

Dependence of women on men was both assumed and assured by legislation that denied to women in the name of the Will of God goods essential to the maintenance of life: property, education, credit, and economic advancement. So engrained became the doctrine of female inferiority as a function of natural law that by the 1860s it was used to validate the "naturalness" of slavery as well (Fitzhugh 249). In fact, when black slavery was instituted in the United States, the laws governing the rights of women in society served as the model for slave laws (Eisler). During the same period, the "white man's burden" became the moral justification for imperialistic agression, and the peoples of other lands submitted to biological and psychological scrutiny which questioned their full human development (Romalis and Romalis 283). Biological determinism held sway. American foreign policy and wars were based on biblical themes of divine election and natural superiority (Chittister). The Roman Catholic Church debated whether or not blacks were fit subjects for ordination, which is to say that the white male Church took seriously the notion that some humans might be less human than other humans. The position was a logical one since it had already been posited that women were lesser creatures, but a discordant one in religious discussion unless that assumption was built into the doctrine, with or without justification by the pristine texts.

In the twentieth century, psychologists wove elaborate schemata designed to distinguish female and male sex differences. Dependence, passivity, emotionalism, compassion, and conformity were female traits; aggression, power, strength, objectivity, and intelligence were male. All of this suited the religious, and male, assumptions that women were by nature inferior (Kagan 39). Given the power to define creation, male literature, research, and legislation created it. God-talk had won again.

Every human institution built inequality into its basic philosophy, operational procedures, and social structures. The fact is that human rights are debatable when the explanation of humanity has a touch of the less than human in it and violence becomes virtue. In military societies, for instance, training programs are geared to "take the woman out of the recruit," to violate the enemy sexually, to link sex and aggression. The U.S. Army marching jingle asserts: "This is my rifle (slapping weapon), this is my gun (slapping crotch). One is for killing, the other for fun" (McAllister). The historical-economic associations between the domination of woman and the making of war are lengthy and obvious. More subtle, more insidious, and more damaging perhaps are the associations between religion, sexism, and war.

Questions and Implications

To this day, two social truths prevail: women are lesser creatures in the eyes of the world, and multiple nations on a small planet see their own needs as rights which are superior to the needs of any of the other peoples of the earth. What is more, nations are willing to subjugate others for their own aggrandizement, even to the point of nuclear obliteration. These two uninterrupted patterns of human behavior need to be explored. Does one reinforce the other? And if so, what is the hope for the resolution of either? More to the point, are institutionalized religion and its creation myths, as they have been traditionally interpreted by the idea agents of each creed, at the very base of this self-destroying pattern?

The interrelationship of sexism, authoritarianism and violence has been long established (McConahay and McConahay;

Divale and Harris). At the same time, every major religion of the world has identified the female element of creation and then proceeded to limit and derogate the nature of women. The question is whether the relationship of theology to sexism and militarism may not be the missing factor in our understanding of the present social moment.

If the theological world view of a people legitimates a theology of domination, do peoples with more benign or less masculine creation myths or imagery — the Taoists and the Puritans, for instance — engage in fewer wars as well as treat women differently? When they do go to war or engage in armed conflict, have they themselves initiated the armed action or are they simply responding to provocation? If so, what does that say about the theories of territorial imperative and violence?

Two concepts confront us: either force negates the possibility of women's ever gaining equality with men, or force may be its own sign of inferiority or underdeveloped humanity. Is the condition of women in society, as well as the occurrence of war, a sign of the real paucity of our presently evolved form as humans? Are present theories of aggression competent to account for the role of religion as a factor in aggression? Modern scholarship has led to the classification of masculine and feminine qualities as patently male and female characteristics. The question to be considered may be whether or not the glorification and institutionalization of the masculine value system may cut off other conflict-resolution options in society and lead to militarism.

By implication, by omission, and by design, religions have provided a construct of life in which God is male, woman's subordination to man is divinely ordained, and woman is by nature either evil or pure, depending on which theological viewpoint you espouse. Religion has been used to assert male superiority and so, by indirection, a theology of domination. Obedience and dominion have been used to justify hierarchy as well as control by the fittest. Therefore, ironically, religion may well lie at the base of both sexism and militarism, since violence done to women legitimates violence done to others.

It is to the effects of this distortion of religious revelation throughout the ages that the Peace Movement must look for the deep, deep linkage between sexism and militarism.

Religion validates violence against women, true. But by implication, these interpretations of the Creation Myth prove implicitly that it is a design of God that some humans are more human than other humans, that some people have been given control of other people, that some people are more god-like than others, that some of creation is inherently bad and must be subjected to others. Inequality, the myths insist, has been built into the human race. Therefore, some people are by nature closer to God; some people are made for others' use; some people but not all people have been "given dominion."

The Theology of Domination — violence, aggression, militarism — becomes logical, necessary, the "white man's burden." In this religious climate, all human rights become debatable. Violence becomes a virtue: the will of God, Armageddon, "Kill a Commie for Christ," Aryan purity.

The point is that the woman's issue is the radical justice issue. If inferiority has been built into the human race by the Creative Principle, then indeed some people have the right and the duty to control all lower levels of life. To believe in the natural inferiority of women is to be just one short step away from the extermination of red people, the segregation of black people, the napalming of yellow people, the exploitation of brown people, the gassing of the next generation of Jews, and now the nuking of the planet. And all in the name of God.

The challenge to the Peace Movement is to see the linkages between sexism, racism, and militarism; to model equality; to gather feminine input to create a new world view; to critique structures in order to change and equalize them; to change sexist language, which, because it excludes women from the mind, excludes them from the real world; to develop conflict-resolution techniques that are feminine; and to call religion to its own best self in living out the doctrines of Baptism, Eucharist, Incarnation, Grace, and Redemption.

Finally, we must retell the Myth.

Both Adam and Eve were made by God as equals, "bone of bone and flesh of flesh."

Neither Adam nor Eve was strong enough to resist temptation.

Both denied the will of God for them in life.

Both were condemned to labor for their sin: she to childbirth and he to work by the sweat of his brow.

Both were excluded from the Garden of Paradise to repair the relationships that they had ruptured, with one another, and with God as a result of their sin.

The purpose of the punishment was to transcend and redeem the sin, not to institutionalize it. We must learn that the violence done to right relationships in the name of God must end before it ends us all.

Bibliography

Ashby, Philip H. *The Conflict of Religions*. New York: Charles Scribner and Sons, 1955.

Bauer, Carol, and Ritt, Lawrence. "A Husband Is a Beating Animal — Frances Power Cobbe Confronts Wife-Abuse Problems in Victorian England." *International Journal of Women's Studies* 6.2,3 (1983).

Buhler, Georg, trans. *The Laws of Manu*. New York: Dover Publications, 1969.

Caplan, Arthur L., ed. *The Sociobiology Debate*. New York: Harper and Row, 1978.

Carmody, Denise Lardner. *Women and World Religions*. Tennessee: Abingdon Press, 1979.

Chittister, O.S.B., Joan D. "Imperialism and the Cold War: a Matter of Motives." Unpublished paper, Penn State University, 1969.

Christopher, John B. *The Islamic Tradition*. New York: Harper and Row, 1972.

Divale, W.F., and Harris, M. "Population, Warfare, and the Male-Supremacist Complex." *American Anthropologist,* 78 (1976): 521-538.

Eisler, Riane. *Dissolution: No-Fault Divorce, Marriage and the Future of Women*. New York: McGraw-Hill, 1977.

Eliade, Mircea. *Patterns in Comparative Religion*. New York: World Publishing Company, 1965.

Fitzhugh, George. "The Failure of Free Society." In *The Annals of America,* Vol. 8. Chicago: Encyclopedia Britannica, Inc., 1968.

Garabedian, John H., and Coombs, Orde. *Eastern Religions in the Electric Age*. New York: Gosset and Dunlap, 1969.

Gottschalk, Louis A., M.D., and Gleser, Goldine C., Ph.D. *The Measurement of Psychological States Through the Content Analysis of Verbal Behavior*. Los Angeles: University of California Press, 1969.

Hole, Judith, and Levine, Ellen. *Rebirth of Feminism*. New York: Quadrangle/The New York Times Book Co., 1975.

Hosken, Fran P. "Female Genital Mutilation and Human Rights." *Feminist Issues: A Journal of Feminist Social and Political Theory,* 1.3 (1981).

Kagan, Jerome. "Check One: Male/Female." *Psychology today,* 3.2 (1969):39.

McAllister, Pam, ed. *Reweaving the Web of Life: Feminism and Non-Violence*. Philadelphia: New Society Publishers, 1982.

McConahay, S., and McConahay, J. "Sexual Permissiveness, Sex-Role Rigidity, and Violence Across Cultures." *Journal of Social Issues*, 2, (1977):134-143.

Miller, Jean Baker, M.D. *Toward a New Psychology of Women*. Boston: Beacon Press, 1976.

Nieboer, Herman. *Slavery as an Industrial System*. New York: B. Franklin, 1971.

Power, Eileen. *Medieval Women*. New York: Cambridge University Press, 1975.

Reuther, Rosemary Radford, ed. *Religion and Sexism*. New York: Simon and Schuster, 1974.

Romalis, Coleman, and Romalis, Shelly. "Sexism, Racism and Technological Change." *International Journal of Women's Studies*, 6.3 (1983):270.

Sanday, Peggy Reeves. *Female Power and Male Dominance*. New York: Cambridge University Press, 1981.

Schaef, Ann Wilson.*Women's Reality*. Minneapolis: Winston Press, 1981.

Straus, Murray, and Gelles, Richard. *Behind Closed Doors*. New York: Doubleday, 1980.

Tavard, George. *Women in Christian Tradition*. South Bend: University of Notre Dame Press, 1973.

10. RELATIONSHIP OF THE NEW CODE OF CANON LAW TO THE DEVELOPMENT OF RELIGIOUS LIFE

Religious life is at a crossroads in time, under pressure from without as well as within. There is, of course, some comfort in the fact that every other human institution is being buffeted as well. Role definitions in marriage are in flux; the scope and authority of government is in question; the boundaries of life are being breached; the very fabric of human and political relations is in tension; the human intelligence has been outraced by its own technology; the very existence of the planet is in danger. The only conclusion is that the world has reached another breakpoint in history. When all institutions at one time are straining to deal with a situation that is impervious to past answers and brimming with new questions, then one era has shifted to another no matter how regretful the passing. In just such moments of history have whole new models of religious life emerged: the eremitical, the cenobitic, the mendicant, the apostolic, and the social service Orders.

Past Paradigms of Religious Life

With the legitimization of Christianity by Constantine, the Fathers and Mothers of the Desert emerged as strong contrasts to the political Christians of the cities who took on the religious practices of their rulers but not always the depth of the faith. To the politicization of the faith, the eremitical life offered a clear call to radical Christian commitment.

Then, with the decline of the Roman Empire cenobitic communities rose up to give focus and stability to the tottering social organization of Western Europe. The eremitical life continued to be revered but ceased to be the prime model for religious life. In the face of social chaos, the religious communities of this time gave to the people of surrounding areas a witness of God's loving care and presence through institutional stability.

When the poor flooded the developing cities in the thirteenth century, mendicant religious followed them, living rootless and poor like the people they served. They challenged with new values an uncaring, urban culture as well as the wealthy establishment church of that period. Monasticism continued to be a gift in the church but the central paradigm of religious life was altered once more.

As the political and religious unity of Europe was shattered by the emergence of nation states and the Protestant schism, new groups of religious now concentrated on the studied articulation and defense of the faith in a divided world. A different form of community lifestyle and organization, not monastic and not local, arose to support this new kind of missionary activity or catechesis and, though each of the other forms remained, this soon became the basic pattern of religious life because of its concentrated focus on the major issues of the time.

Finally, with the massive emigration of Europeans to the United States and the world-wide influence of the French Revolution on its press for equal rights, six hundred new religious congregations arose in the eighteenth century to soften the effects of an enslaving industrialization by acts of mercy and to insert ghetto outsiders into a strange culture by educating the outcast Catholic for public service in a white, Anglo-Saxon, Protestant culture. Religious became identified by the institutionalized services they gave to such an extent that vocation and work began to be seen as identical.

The point is that religious communities have always fundamentally been signs of God's loving concern, not in a passive way, not by running away from the issues or problems of the period, but by confronting them directly. Though the commitment to the Christ of the Gospel remained always the same, in moments of major upheaval as universal issues changed, so did the style or focus of religious life in order to deal with these issues, despite the fact that in many instances these very changes invariably caused conflict in the church.

The problem is that we face new issues now. The massive destruction of peoples, the exploitation of the poor, the oppression of women, the breakdown of community, the control of the world and its resources, the diminishment of the intrinsic value of the human being, the global struggle for equality and systemic participation are all questions that cry to the Gospel for judgment.

Religious of this generation stand half way between two eras. On the one hand, there is a new Gospel agenda in our time for which old institutions are largely insufficient. On the other, there are the expectations and responsibilities that are the price of past success. The questions are: What does the future look like? What model of religious life is needed to address it? and Does the new Code of Canon Law enable or obstruct the attempt?

Present Pressures on the Future of Religious Life

If the function of religious life is to give witness to the Gospel in the present age, it is important to reflect on the characteristics of the present social situation that call for Gospel witness.

In the first place science has developed a momentum and a morality of its own. Human engineering, military technology, and global control far outstrip the ethics of another age. Learning from the past has become a thing of the past. The future has become a research laboratory in which what can be done will be done, regardless of whether it is blessing or boon. And the people are the last to know or to understand or to be considered. Interpretation and evaluation become in this environment the very basics of life. When science outstrips ethics, without guidance there are only two choices: surrender or reactionism. And neither is acceptable.

At the same time, the world has come to a hot, focused point where communication is instant and anger is instant and annihilation is instant. Everything is open and immediate and local now. The same pair of shoes, the same car, the same computer are made in five parts of the world at once. Everything is linked: resources and economy and people. Industrialism has been shifted to the Third World. Money and power are in the North. A young, young world is rising in the Southern hemisphere. But who and what will integrate it all before the strain becomes too much for the present situation to bear?

Furthermore, individualism and autonomy have become high level issues across the globe. Participation in decision-making has become an expectation, not a privilege. The smallest of groups want their independence and their vote in the United Nations. OPEC and the Arab League and the Contadoras and the PLO all rise to challenge the domination of the post World War II world. These days people expect to be self-directing and equal, whatever their wealth, whatever their size. It is not that they do not want government; they want government of their own making. Independence, interdependence, and equality have become the fragile touchstones of a developing world, sparing no persons and no institutions.

Finally, in the midst of all these social realities, the Church has come to define itself as part of, rather than separate from, the culture around it. Consequently, it is rediscovering its role as leaven and salt rather than as City of God under siege. The theology of transcendence has given way to a theology of transformation that has touched religious communities deeply. Above and beyond cosmetic changes, whole charisms are still in the process of being traced and tested because life has changed around, as well as within, religious institutions. At this crossover point in history, it is once again the very focus of religious life that is at issue. The basic church question has become whether or not religious renewal means a modified version of the past or a largely new kind of commitment within past principles. The question is not academic; many fundamental shifts have already occurred within communities and been approved by their own chapter bodies on the basis of their evaluation of the signs of the times.

The Relation of the Signs of the Times to the Model of Religious Life

In a culture where science is not only value-free but often valueless, the world may not so much need those who give standard educational answers as it needs someone to rely on to press hard philosophical questions. To teach science is one thing. To ask whether that which is scientifically, socially, or economically possible is also morally appropriate is entirely another. But with this realization comes an even clearer one: religious must confront the notion of institutionalism-for-its-own-sake. It is not enough to simply run alternative organizations in a world where social services have in most places become part of the fabric of society. The great religious founders created systems for the church that were sorely needed. They did not duplicate old models; they gave the society new ones. In our own times, the same thing may be happening. But the greatest difficulty facing this generation of religious in their attempt to relate to these times may well be the success of the last.

With operational costs rising and population and personnel declining, some previously flourishing institutions are clearly nonviable. In fact, a proper stewardship of resources indicates that some of these must be and need to be closed or the energy and vision of communities may well be poured out on the tasks of the past rather than on the challenges of the present. Just because a community has always had a school or a hospital is no sign that it should have one now, even if it can afford to. The function of the religious institution is not to be viable; it is to be prophetic.

The implications are obvious. In the future, not all religious will be in institutionalized ministries. In some instances, the institutions themselves will disappear; in others, religious will have to choose to minister in those public arenas where national, social, economic, and legislative agendas can be subject to the moral critique of the Gospel and where the voice of the voiceless can be heard through them. Moreover, in a culture where globalism is a fact of daily life, religious institutions must be centers devoted to world peace, to equality, to social justice, and to Christian reflection on these issues. Otherwise, our only sign may well be the sign of failure to attend to the contemporary human agenda from a Christian perspective.

Finally, in the surging search for human rights and equality as Gospel standards, religious communities themselves must be signs of full life in Christ or the Good News itself will come into question. The Church cannot call others to what it does not model or practice itself.

The question is whether or not the new code sustains these efforts by religious to attend to the new needs of the time while dealing with the attendant reality of the aging of their membership, the decline of their institutions, and questions about the authenticity of their charisms.

The New Code of Canon Law and Religious Life

The new code of canon law for religious is a rare blend of past and future, many times in contention, often in synergy. The model of community, authority, ministry, and church that emerges in the canons seems to recognize the possibility that new needs might emerge, that authority is to be shared, that community is essential, and that the church is a body of adult believers with gifts. At the same time, there is an underlying sense that vision is not in vogue. At the level of principle, the code is expansive. At the level of practice, the new code often sets perimeters from the past. Point: the effects of the new law on emerging models of authority, ministry, community, and church are mixed.

Authority. On the questions of responsibility in the church, the code takes two positions: decentralization and clericalism. One advances the quest for autonomy and participation considerably; the other may well serve to keep it in check.

Over and over again, the new code sets universal norms but explicitly states that the constitutions of a congregation can decree otherwise or at least modify the norms according to what is "proper to the institute." More than that, processes once controlled precisely by Rome — exclaustration, election procedures, organizational structures, enclosure, terms of office, visitation, the use and administration of goods — have been ceded to local community authority. Subsidiarity, in other words, is a very real dimension of a law framed in the spirit of Vatican II.

The new code, for instance, gives to religious institutes themselves the right to suppress or divide sections or units of the congregation or federation or Order. This right of local authorities to move quickly to authenticate or absorb parts of the congregational structure can have at least two effects. In the first place, the group itself, who can best recognize not only a geographical shift in ministry but also the psychological value of its validation, will enjoy the flexibility of group development. In the second place, long-range planning to avoid the impression of the deterioration of religious life will become both easier and imperative. In the United States where the total number of religious has declined from 176,000 in 1962 to 96,000 in 1983, this local control may well be key to the continued revitalization of religious life. The image of half-empty monasteries is no sign of religious vitality and ought to be avoided like the plague. Commitment, not numbers, is the key to religious witness, and as ministries and membership profiles change, congregations must move quickly to become disengaged from past institutions which are a drain on the resources and energy of a community.

The fact that leaves of absence, exclaustrations, transfers, and even dispensations to a certain degree are also now given to the local level to grant gives a clearer picture of the nature of the relationships involved. Religious professions have never been registered in Rome, only dispensations. There is something wrong with a system that recognizes people only when they leave it. The new code reflects the realization that bonds forged in the community ought to be dissolved there so that everyone concerned realizes that the rupture is personal rather than simply legal. In this capacity then, the new law is indeed a truer and clearer image of the theology of community life itself.

At the same time that the code shifts this locus of responsibility, however, it does not do much to alter the hierarchical theology of obedience and authority. The model of a church of believing but ordered adults waits in the wings of this document. Neither the language of obedience nor the mode of authority as it is expressed in the code suggests much development. "Superiors" are to govern their "subjects" as "children" of God, though in the spirit of service and for voluntary obedience (c. 618). "Consultative and participatory bodies" are assumed — an advance in structure indeed — but "wise discernment" is to be used in their establishment and use (c. 633.2). The feeling is that such groups are normative but suspect, rather than necessary or even of the essence of Christian leadership. The strong call for participation and personal responsibility that might be expected both from the Acts of the Apostles as well as Vatican II and contemporary culture is absent from any discussion of authority in this code. As a result the emergence of team governments in religious institutes is denied by virtue of the fact that authority is presumed to reside in a single person, a notion foreign both to the history of the early Church and the present culture.

Most limiting of all is the continued insistence on priestly or-

dination and therefore maleness, as the basis for church governance (c. 129.1). Decision-making in church governance is simply denied to the non-ordained, though participation in church
ministry is encouraged (c. 394.2,511). Certainly, the failure to
see this call to contribute to the apostolate of the church as a
breakthrough, however limited, is to ignore history. Nevertheless, the reality remains that though lay people and women may
work in the church, the church clearly belongs to someone else.
In every human institution, people seek civil rights and the
church speaks in their support. In divine institutions, it seems,
basic rights do not apply. In the Church, men write all the
policies, men define all the positions, and men elect only other
men to continue the system. The effect of this exclusion on religious life itself, on women, on people looking for signs of human
dignity in Christianity, and on the credibility of the Church's
definition of itself is yet to be seen in a world where autonomy,
equality, and human rights have the highest priority.

Ministry. Some of the most impelling sections of the code deal
with ministry. Lay institutes of men and women "participate in
the pastoral mission of the Church through the spiritual and
corporal works of mercy, performing very many different services for people," the canon reads (c. 676). Women religious, of
course, are in a no-choice situation. Ordination and its basis for
full ministry in the church is closed to them, including the
deaconal state for which there is precedent in history. Women
and their communities have no direct access to God, but must
have the Eucharist mediated to them by males who have no
identity with the particular ecclesial community other than as
ritual functionary. The liturgical theology of this position is, of
course, obscure. On the other hand, male religious may have
just as much of a struggle with what it means to be both clerical
and religious. Which call has priority, and what effect that duality has on both their personal identity and their fundamental
option for religious life has very real meaning for the development of male communities of religious. If community life itself
is a valuable witness in the church, then what is the reason for

the clericalization of male communities? And if the reason is to make full Christian community possible, then what does that say for the spiritual quality of women's communities?

At the same time, there are hopeful signs in the new code for the developing role of the laity, and therefore many religious, in the ministry of the church. Multiple avenues of new ministry for lay religious — spiritual direction, retreat work, parish administration, preaching, and liturgical service — become possible at least by implication as a result of this code (c. 230.2, 517.2, 758, 766, 861.2, 910.2, 943, 1112.1,.2). With the decline in the number of priests, these opportunities may well become the basis for an entirely different type of participation by religious in the ministry of the church.

Clearly, the code is also in creative tension with itself. The bishop is told quite clearly to foster various forms of the apostolate, "according to the needs of the place or time" (c. 394.2) and even to collaborate with religious in the discernment of these services (c. 678.3). Religious, however, are to "hold fast to the mission and works which are proper to their institute" and "prudently to adapt them" (c. 677.1). Only creative interpretation in a period of great change will protect this canon from itself. At the same time, the key to the reconciliation of these two positions — to provide for new needs but not to depart from past services — may be the call to consultation, rather than direction, between bishops and religious about the works to be done (c. 678.3). Where adaptation of ministry also involves the alienation of property, however, the rights of bishops to deter diocesan communities in this regard is a potential source of additional tension and control (c. 1292.1). The subject is crucial to the ongoing development of religious life. It is exactly the standardization and ossification of the religious works of the immediate past that have made both renewal and relevance the difficult tasks they are. So wedded have we become to our traditional works that adaptation has been often unthinkable.

The exclusion of religious from participation in civil authority

(c. 672/285.3) limits for this period what had been a common practice in the history of Western Europe before this century. The important thing to remember is that this restriction of religious from the exercise of civil authority or power ought not to be read to mean that religious are excluded from exerting influence on public or political issues. Holding political office and functioning in the political arena are two entirely different things; the distinction is crucial in a period where legislative reform may be essential to the on-going existence of the human race. If the two are confused, then we may well be abandoning the public forum at a moment in history when it has never needed the critique of the Gospel more. In fact one of the more exciting calls of the code to religious is its injunction for communities as communities to "donate something from their own resources to help the needs of the church and the support of the poor" (c. 640). "Witness" and prayer and concern, it seems, are not enough in a day when the foundations of society are under stress.

Community. It is in the area of community life itself that the new code is most regressive and contradictory, where breakthroughs are lacking, and where, therefore, the future of religious life may well be most endangered.

The concept of unique charisms is affirmed in the code time after time (c. 577, 578). Nevertheless, one mode of life is required of all traditions, both monastic and apostolic. In each, community is clearly defined as the common life, the Liturgy of the Hours as the standard prayer form, a habit as the essential sign of commitment and poverty (c. 607.2, 665.1, 663.3, 669.1).

These specifications present multiple problems for the development of a religious life for this time. In the first place, since the law is careful to record that everything stated applies equally to both men and women, unless otherwise indicated, the assumption is that male clerical religious who for long years have lived alone for parish work, special ministries, or missionary activities will also now be collected into living groups. Otherwise someone is going to have to answer why women religious from the same spiritual traditions cannot do the same.

Secondly, the Liturgy of the Hours, a choral prayer, necessarily limits if not the prayer quality of non-monastic communities at least their form, size, and ministries. The idea that all religious must pray a choral office may be not only impossible but also undesirable for apostolic orders for whom a monastic prayer life could be a disservice to the full emergence of their unique charism.

Finally, the requirement of a uniform habit raises the whole issue not only of the social-psychological effects of uniforms but, especially in Protestant countries or in nations where the separation of church and state has high priority, of the ability of religious to leaven the public sector or to earn the monies necessary to maintain themselves and expand their services to the poor. The Church, after all, has come to define itself as part of, rather than separate from the culture around it. Given that perspective, many groups have relinquished a uniform or traditional religious habit in order to walk among people in a manner more like the Christ of Emmaus than the Christ of the Transfiguration. They have opened their communities to non-members, become part of people's lives and made others part of theirs. They have found ministry outside of their own institutions and often outside of the Catholic structure itself. All of those things are not just departures from the past; they are also shapers of the future.

The homogenization of religious institutes is not totally without merit, however, if the elimination of "higher" and "lower" orders — a recognition of the "religious" character of congregations devoted to apostolic work — does not also suppress the full development of the apostolic spirituality of these groups. The concern of St. Vincent de Paul echoes ominously; he warned against practices and lifestyles that would make ministry impossible. The realization that apostolic spirituality is unique is long overdue.

Obstacles and Invitations to the Development of Religious Life

Dependence, conformity, and institutionalized functionalism were hallmarks of pre-Vatican II religious life. The new code, at least in embryo if not with enthusiasm, can enable us to go beyond that level of human development and service, a development sorely needed if the tide and tempo of these times are to take seriously the presence of the church. Responsibility, community-building, and discernment of gifts are the emerging ideals. The new code may not make a clarion call for these qualities. But the seeds are there for those who have the courage to use the authority given them to shape for the church the new models of community, prayer, and ministry that can speak to the modern world. The clear feeling is that the present code is not enough for this time but it certainly gives broader, deeper scope than ever before. Within it is at least the outline of a new kind of authority and ministry. For those for whom charism and contemporary service are imperatives, that in itself is a promising beginning.

11. AMERICAN WOMEN RELIGIOUS AND MINISTRY: NEW CHALLENGE, TRADITIONAL RESPONSE

The renewal of Roman Catholic religious life for women has taken many turns in the last twenty years. The lifestyle, governance models, prayer forms, formation criteria and theology of the vows which directed the life of women religious in this century have all been scrutinized in an attempt to make the life both relevant to today's needs and faithful to the original inspiration of religious orders. Changes have been widespread and critical. But it is not in these isolated pieces that the effects of renewal come into focus. It is in the ministries that now flow from religious life that the quality of renewal is most clear.

Nineteenth century religious life was a common life of regulated behaviors and work that functioned to maintain the institution but not necessarily to bring each woman to fullness of human growth and potential. Nevertheless, at the same time that nuns were being taught their functionalism, they were also getting a clear, if unconscious, awareness of their effectiveness as well. Almost the entire social-service network of the Catholic Church in the United States was owned and/or operated by communities of women religious for over 150 years, accountable to the Church but most often operationally independent of it. With their own money and with their own personnel, religious built and staffed most of the Catholic colleges, academies, hospitals, orphanages, and special-care facilities in the country. The self-understanding that emerged from these experiences was in direct contradiction to the values and standards imbued in their formation programs. As administrators they were designing programs worth thousands of dollars; in their convents they were asking permission to read the newspaper. In their personal lives they were treated as children; in their apostolic activities they needed initiative, vision, a sense of risk, competence, confidence, assertiveness, independence, and community corroboration. Moreover, they needed, and got, high-level professional educations. It was to these experiences of achievement, self-direction, and mutual support as well as to the fundamental theology of religious life and the histories of their Orders that women religious turned eventually for renewal and redefinition.

Just as firmly as they moved to eliminate authoritarianism, depersonalization, and conformity from their lives, American women religious began to question their works as well. Most religious communities had been called to this country by American bishops to minister to Catholic immigrant populations under the auspices of a given diocese. They were expected to be self-supporting but at the service of the local Church and under its authority. Out of this system had arisen the entire Catholic institutional system.

By the 1960s the effects of common works, control and economic pressure had begun to take a heavy toll. The specialization of all areas of ministry — education, health care, and social service work — made it increasingly difficult to treat women religious as a collection of interchangeable parts. Being put into positions for which they were not prepared or for which they had little talent or interest was beginning to affect women's very commitment to the religious life. Of those who left convents at this time, many said that it was because they could not be themselves. What is more, the stipends provided women religious were far below the national minimum wage. In 1966, the average sister's stipend in the parochial school system was $100 per month, without benefit of health insurance or retirement monies. Many are barely above that even now. Nevertheless, women religious provided their own food, shelter, health care, and education with the exception of local convents provided for Sisters working in the parishes. Consequently, as transportation, insurance, and professional education costs became compulsory and increasingly higher, religious women could actually no longer afford to restrict themselves to parochial ministry. Finally, the whole philosophical question of justice and the role of women in society became a critical one.

Over three-quarters of the 1500 respondents from 23 communities who participated in a 1978 Ministry Survey argued that since the religious community reflects the Church, it must therefore be outgoing and open to the secular, and that furthermore, non-institutional ministries provide a dynamic way to respond to the needs of the times. What may be even more important is the fact that over 90 percent of the respondents rejected the traditional concept that the best work a religious community can do will take the form of an institutional corporate apostolate under the guidance of the hierarchy. Finally, this group argued that their community leaders should enable the development of new community ministries and themselves speak out on social issues. This confluence of circumstances, social change, and a new theology of church brought women religious to decisions that altered the structures but not the direction of their lives. More than that, it altered their modes of service in contemporary society.

Having said all that about the history, culture, and circumstances that surround the ministries of women religious in this country, the fact remains that basically little has changed where the works of religious are concerned. The work of American women religious has historically been devoted to the needs of the oppressed and the poor. Today, American religious are simply turning once again to the needs of the new poor.

Women religious came to this country to minister to the needs of a large, basically poor, Catholic population in a then largely Protestant country. Language was a major barrier to both employment, advancement,and enculturation. Education appeared to be the answer and parochial schools the way to maintain religious beliefs and practices and to eventually insert Catholic citizens into the white, Anglo-Saxon, Protestant culture around them. By the time John F. Kennedy took the presidential oath of office in this country, that task had been largely accomplished, at least for that population. The schools were established, and generations of the laity had been prepared to staff and direct the schools as well as to value them. The Catholic population as a whole had been assimilated into mainstream America and, like it, had moved to the suburbs. The question now became: Who would care for those left behind and how?

It was the late 1960s: The Vietnam War raged; blacks staged sit-ins at lunch counters in the South; Watts burned; public politicians lied and cheated; new classes of immigrants began to pour into the United States; the Women's Movement exposed the discrimination that came with being born female; the United States pursued militarism with a vengeance. In the midst of all this, Vatican Council II called for the renewal of religious life according to "the charism of the order, the intentions of the founder, and the signs of the times." Business-as-usual simply wasn't working anymore. Women religious began to move from classrooms to soup kitchens, to neighborhood action centers, to public welfare programs, to legal aid offices, to pastoral teams in parishes, to diocesan peace and justice offices, to safe-houses for battered women. At the same time, it is important to remember, many did not move out of classrooms at all. They stayed in education but changed textbooks and curricula to deal with the problems of the time or they became involved on a spare-time basis with advocacy groups that were themselves organized to address these issues. Whole communities adopted corporate commitments to specific social questions — housing, nuclear disarmament, poverty, justice — and pledged themselves to promote these questions wherever each of them might be: in education, in health care institutions, in office work, in either the private or parochial sector. Some Sisters deliberately sought full-salaried, high-paying positions so that other members of the community could work directly with and for people or organizations who could not afford to pay for services at all.

Sisters who were being blamed, in other words, for abandoning the Catholic school system were simply doing what had always been done in the best tradition of religious life and in the immediate history of their own communities: they were bringing the Gospel to bear on the issues of the time; they were standing with and for the new poor; they were standing between two cultures with one foot firmly planted in each. They were now, however, as intent on removing the obstacles to justice as they were to doing charity.

Nevertheless, real pressures and obstructions exist. The transition has been no easier for the religious of this century than it was for the pioneers of the last. Many communities owned buildings that housed previous ministries but were yet unpaid for; most religious had standard educational degrees and had to be prepared in whole new fields; many communities themselves were situated far away from the new problems and the new poor; community schedules and living patterns were strained in the attempts to respond; the structures unique to apostolic religious life for women — companions, community life, hours of work — had to be questioned; the mortgages and populations and facilities of times past were with them still while new needs arose on every side.

The price of transition is external as well. Identification with the middle class makes identification with the poor difficult for religious, too. Most of today's religious were formed in middle class houses, with middle-class lives and middle-class expectations of education and hot water and cars and full meals. It is not always possible to make the adjustment to a ghetto lifestyle. Knowing this, however, many religious women who cannot live with the poor live for the poor as advocates, as researchers, as activists, as a social conscience and voice for the voiceless.

The residual theology of pre-Vatican II religious life, the notion that the function of religious life is to transcend the world, to be outside of it, to withdraw from it, is still a force in the Church, in society, and in some religious themselves. The "witness" mythology of separation, designed to ground the religious spiritually and to enable the religious to avoid chaotic activism, has too often led religious to opt for empty symbolism or fabricated pieties instead of the real thing. It is not enough to say the Stations of the Cross when the oppressed in our own towns have no one to go before the judges for them. The function of religious ministry today is to move again from subjective signs of personal commitment to objective transformation of the society by bringing the Good News to our own times. The function of religious life is to transform the world and to bring the foolish standards of the Gospel to the issues of the age.

The definition of religious life by task, as teachers or nurses, rather than as disciples sent to proclaim, reduces the prophetic function of religious life, domesticates it, institutionalizes it, muzzles it. It leads people to ask seriously, "But should a religious be in a public demonstration? Should a religious be lobbying? Should a religious be involved in political issues?" We have so sanctified the separation of church and state that it has become an evil in this society for a Christian to call the conscience of the king.

Women religious of this period have borne all of these burdens of transition with hope. They go on using their existing institutions for both new and old ministries; they have become a Christian presence in other ones; they have chosen to be leaven as well as labor force. They have become centers of community, consciousness, influence, relinquishment, and critical clarity to call and to question.

There are some who say that the aging of communities of women religious is a sure sign of their death, but I am not convinced. Where life and commitment converge, age is no factor. The scripture reads that when the angel-guests who had yielded to their insistent hospitality told Abraham and old Sarah she would bear a child. Sarah laughed. Yet from her came the beginning of a whole new people. *Perfectae caritatis*, the Vatican II decree on the renewal of religious life, reads: "A life consecrated by a profession of the counsels is of surpassing value and has a necessary role to play in the circumstances of the present age." Our challenge is to minister insistently in hope and beyond hope, knowing that in and through the most impossible circumstances God will work God's will.

12. ROME AND RELIGIOUS LIFE: A MATTER OF PERSPECTIVES

"Progress might have been all right once, but it's gone on too long." That sentence was written by Ogden Nash. It could have been written by Rome.

After almost twenty years of the constitutional renewal that had been mandated of religious orders by Vatican II and guided by the General Chapters of all religious communities, a new document from the Congregation for Religious, directed specifically and first to American Religious, has appeared that brings the Vatican II renewal of religious life in conflict with current Vatican norms. This document, entitled, "Essential Elements in the Church's Teaching on Religious Life," deals with the theological nature of religious consecration and then with its "characteristics." It is at the level of characteristics that two distinctly different visions of religious life emerge: one, the pattern of renewal communities in the United States; the other, the Roman model. Vatican II asked religious some questions about charism and spirit and the needs of the members and the signs of the times. The "Essential Elements" document implies that someone else knew the answers all the time and that American religious have not discovered the right ones. What was thought to be a journey of experimentation, update, and renewal has turned out to be an Easter egg hunt. The result is deep theological tension between the Curia and American women religious that demands dialogue. The resolution of the two viewpoints is imperative if religious life is to maintain its prophetic presence in the Church. This paper is an attempt to describe these two perspectives.

The questions are: What are the bases for the differences and what are their implications?

Five major issues, I believe, underlie the tension between Rome and, in particular, U.S. women religious: attitudes toward law, concepts of authority, the meaning of witness, assumptions about lifestyle and the role of women. None is independent of the others. All in fact reflect the struggle between the theology of transcendence and the theology of transformation that now touches the Church in every aspect. Moreover, at these points of intersection may well rest the future of religious life for women in the United States.

As the constitutions of American communities of women religious are submitted to Rome for approval, certain concerns emerge again and again in the CRIS (Congregation for Religious and Secular Institutes) critiques, regardless of community history or charism. The common life, common works, common prayer, common dress, common devotions, and the centralized or personal authority of superiors are the constants. Each of these elements was standard fare for pre-Vatican II religious life. Each of them has been at least modified in most U.S. religious congregations since. Whether the differences between the constitutional norms of American religious and the standards set by the Vatican are cosmetic or essential, cultural or theological, fundamental or superficial remains to be seen. One thing is certain, however; the differences reflect two entirely distinct world-views.

Attitudes toward Law

To the Roman mind, the function of law is to define the ideal. Dispensation is the device used to adjust the desirable to the attainable. Dispensation is a sign of adaptation.

To the American mind, on the other hand, the function of law is to define the normative. Americans write the minimum of law for the maximum of people. In this world-view, the desirable is attainable or it would not have been required in the first place. Dispensation is seen as deviance, as weakness, as unwanted or unwarranted exception.

The differences are more than rhetorical, more than philosophical, more than academic. They account in large part for the reluctance of American religious to accept some of the items they are being directed to include in their revised congregational constitutions.

For instance, the "Essential Elements" and the canons as well say that devotion to the Blessed Virgin is a necessary part of religious life and that daily Eucharist is essential. But for those Orders in which Marian devotion is not part of the spiritual tradition or for the many for whom daily Eucharist is impossible, the call to include these items in the Constitutions is at least formation in false conscience or, worse, an inauthentic expression of life as they know it to be.

Again and again, while women religious insist that they cannot include prescriptions that do not have an essential place in their lives, Curial officers insist that they must, on the understanding that they do what they can and request dispensations or permission to account for circumstances that make the ideal impossible. To American women religious, to write something down that you know you cannot do or do not do or will not do is dishonest. To the Curia, to omit it is to institutionalize decadence.

Attitudes toward Authority

In pre-Vatican II communities of women religious of the nineteenth and twentieth centuries, all authority was seen as given by God for the direction of others in hierarchical fashion: first, to the Pope and civil officials and then, through them, to bishops, pastors, and other "duly constituted superiors" whose positions had been confirmed by proper institutional authority. Superiors, since they shared in the authority of God, were understood to have a God-given right and duty to control and judge the lives of others. In religious communities of women this direction translated into the minute details of life. Sisters were assigned to their work — e.g., teaching, nursing, or domestic management — without benefit of consultation or personal orientation because the virtue of obedience superseded all other qualities, a factor not without parallel in the lives of other women as well. As a result their works, gifts and talents were seriously circumscribed. They knelt before the superior, as before a feudal lord, to ask permission for even the most essential details of life with the formula, "For the love of Jesus, Sister, may I have shoelaces, work in my classroom on Saturday, go to the dentist, wash my clothes." A sense of dependence permeated every element of life. Rule books, custom books and ceremonials regulated the woman's life throughout every activity of the day: eating, praying, dressing, walking, and talking. Most important, the women superiors who were charged with guarding the observance of their communities were themselves subject to men of the Church for the approbation or amendment of these practices, most of which had in fact been written by men. For men alone had access to both the education and the authority of the Church, and it was before men that women knelt to make their Order's vows. By the twentieth century, women religious made few, if any, decisions on their own.

Of all the efforts of renewal, new approaches to authority were perhaps the most meaningful. Sisters had been trained to be dependent and were told that this was a virtue, since sin left the human being, and especially women, inherently weak and in need of enlightened external direction. But as a result of renewal, responsible obedience rather than blind obedience became the norm. In the face of the history of women's communities, the democratic environment of the United States, the educational level of their members, and the call of the Church itself in Vatican II for collegiality and subsidiarity, communities of American women religious simply asserted the position that self-direction was possible to women and at the same time not inimical to religious life. In the light of these new understandings, women religious have rewritten their own constitutions, often contrary to and independent of past documents that were written or shaped for them almost entirely by men.

The renewed insistence on local superiors and of "a life largely laid down for them," and the notion that authority does not reside in the community itself nor derive from the members themselves but is only "conferred by the Church" raises major theological questions about the role and function of the Holy Spirit in the Christian community. It also raises the spectre once again of infantilism, dependence, and conformity rather than the mutual listening that obedience has come to imply.

The authority of the Pope is not in question. However, the requirement that obedience to the Pope as the immediate superior of every religious must be written into every Constitution in addition to its proper place in Canon Law, for instance, is seen as an instance of selective emphasis of the canons. The repetition is proper to Jesuits perhaps, but less a focus of other Orders and so represents a skewing of the charism and purpose of Congregations that derive from other traditions which can conceivably affect their direction or structures in the future.

Shared authority, team government, the discernment process, the prophetic call — all pale in the light of this approach. Furthermore, the experiences of the last twenty years that have been discovered to be life-giving and dynamic are apparently being ignored. To withdraw from these now in favor of a chain-of-command type of obedience is seen by the women as more military than ecclesial. Not to reassert the form is seen by Rome as infidelity. To the American religious, such a position is equivalent to saying that those governments that are not monarchies are not governments.

Attitudes toward Witness

Religious work and religious garb are the two horns of this dilemma. Rome wants religious communities to identify their apostolates and to maintain the traditional ones. The works are to be "mandated." American women religious see social-cultural needs to which the Gospel must be brought but for which no institutions exist: the hungry on the city streets of the United States, the sexually abused, the addicted, the poor without voice, the minorities without influence, the need for demilitarization. At the same time, American women also know the burden and trap that institutions can be. Large buildings and large debts are both the inheritance of the success of the past and an obstacle to the future. Rome wants American communities to name their apostolates. The document reads: "In the case of other institutes — those not clerical or missionary — working alone is with the permission of superiors to meet an exceptional need for a certain time." American religious want to follow the gifts of their members under the rubric of peace and justice. They want to enable their members to be what they have the gift to be rather than be interchangeable parts of a single machine, but at the same time to work for peace and justice whatever their position. That philosophy often entails working alone with groups and people who are not "brothers or sisters of the same religious family," or of any religious family for that matter.

In order to do these things, religious uniform needs to be optional. Some religious work in public positions in order to enable other members of the congregation to work for little or nothing, including in the Catholic school system. If the Church is to be leaven in a non-Catholic world, its religious must be able to move from group to group with ease. The Jesus of Emmaus must be as acceptable as the Jesus of the Transfiguration.

Rome, it seems, sees the Church as a place to which people come. American religious have come to see the Church as a people to whom the Church must go. The distinction in those two types of witness is crucial. It is not that one is better than the other. The fact is simply that both must be affirmed.

Attitudes toward Lifestyle

In 1545 the Council of Trent, the counter-Reformation ecumenical council of the Roman Catholic Church, attempted to offset Protestant criticism and scandal over the breakdown of convent discipline that came as a result of either the concentration of wealth among the nuns of noble birth or the dire poverty in convents that accompanied the Black Death. Trent gave bishops the right to conduct episcopal visitations in communities of nuns as delegates of the Holy See and, even more conclusive, forbade women religious to leave the enclosure of their monasteries without permission of the bishop or, in some cases, of the Pope. This total restriction of movement curtailed their works, their influence and their personal development. Four factors dominated nineteenth-century convent life: it was at least "semi-cloistered," it was highly authoritarian and functional in nature, it put a premium on anonymity, and it precluded personal relationships. Consequently, one of the most serious of the questions asked during the renewal period of communities of American women religious was whether or not the common life could also be a community life.

With the abandonment of practices that controlled their social relations — the inspection of mail, the limitation of visiting hours and secular reading materials, the companion-system, and semi-cloister — women religious took to themselves the right to function in the public arena as adults and to form networks that would affect both their apostolic activities and their social influence. The phenomenon of enclosure for women was officially rejected by the women themselves. Small group living and individual living conditions, to which male members of apostolic religious Orders had been accustomed for years, became commonplace. The "Essential Elements" document restates the concept that religious life requires "sharing of prayer, work, meals, and leisure lived in a community of the institute under the authority of a local superior." Travel, social contacts, and use of the media are matters of religious obedience, the document states.

The whole question, of course, is how much openness a group can have and still remain a group. But artificial society is no substitute for community either. Army bases and prisons attest to that. American women religious feel they are well on their way to finding the balance in community life between extreme conformity on the one hand and extreme individualism on the other. A new era of pseudo-monasticization is certainly not the answer in a culture that is far-flung in both its needs and its options.

Attitudes toward Women

Basic to each of these issues is the emerging sense of the full personhood of woman that is developing, at least theoretically, in our time. The philosophy of dualism has been basic to the role of women in society and to the development of religious life for women. The continual emphasis on self-repression which existed in convents of the pre-Vatican II era was a direct expression of a male theology and philosophy that regarded women, by virtue of their sexual function, as the manifestation of unintelligent carnality. The scholastic philosopher Thomas Aquinas (1225-1274) wrote: "Sobriety is most requisite in the young and in women, because concupiscence of pleasure thrives in the young on account of the heat of youth, while in women there is not sufficient strength of mind to resist concupiscence;" and again, "Man is yet further ordered to a still nobler vital action (than woman) and that is intellectual operation."[1]

Out of this cultural and theological sense of the valuelessness, inadequacy, or inherent undiscipline of women came religious practices that struck at the very identity of the woman religious. She assumed a new name, often that of a male saint; she wore

clothes designed to obliterate any sense of her femaleness; she
forfeited the right to personal initiative or self-direction; and,
what's more, heard all of these postures reinforced in the documents of the Church on religious life. The prayers put on her lips
in official texts told her that women saints — women, in other
words, whom the Church held up as approved and to be emu-
lated — were women noted for their docility, humility, submissiveness, and virginity. Finally, though they devoted themselves to religious perfection all of their lives, women religious
were never considered capable of interpreting, defining, or
structuring their own life situations. On the contrary, those
tasks were reserved to male spiritual directors, canonists, and
theologians, all of which positions were closed to women by the
canons of the Church. Womanhood had become a thing of weakness and women religious its most schooled example.

One of the by-products of renewal, in fact, was the reestablish-
ment of the personal identity of the woman religious and the development of an environment where the emergence of individu-
ality was a strength rather than a threat to the ongoing
dynamism of the group. The institutionalism and depersonalization common to all women, but to women religious in a special
way, was dealt a death blow with the elimination of uniform
dress and restrictive social controls. Not only did religious
women begin to see themselves in new ways as a result but they
also began to interact with other persons and institutions differently.

And that is precisely the problem. American women religious
have come of age. They want to be seen as equals, to be treated
as equals, to minister as equals, and to participate in the decision-making processes of their lives as equals. They are not
claiming to be right; they are claiming to be full human beings,
self-directing persons, adults.

In research conducted among women religious of this decade,
a conscious rejection of the traditional theology of woman was
clear.[2] The group considered the role of women in the Church

and took the following positions: Almost all (87 percent) reject the Thomistic position that men as men are clearer images of God than women are. Most (87 percent) believe that effective parish team ministry should include women. Nearly two-thirds (64 percent) believe that their communities should call for a wider representation of women on pontifical, ecclesiastical and diocesan commissions. Over half (57 percent) believe that women who work with the broken, the sick, and the dying should be able to administer the sacraments of healing and reconciliation. Nearly half (49 percent) believe that they have a responsibility to call leaders to accountability when they select men over equally qualified women for positions in the Church. Over half (56 percent) do not believe that when men are present, they should be given preference over women in exercising liturgical functions (as readers, cantors, or ministers of the Eucharist, for instance.) A significant portion (39 percent) believe they have an obligation to support qualified women who seek ordination, though only 16 percent say that they themselves want to be ordained.

The evolution of this kind of consciousness spells a period of philosophical tension for the Church. The problem between Rome and American women religious is much deeper than simply the approval of new Constitutions. The problem has something to do with being religious, with being person, with being Church that is new for our time, that is not going to go away.

NOTES

[1]Aquinas, Thomas, *Summa Theologica,* Vol. 1, II, Qu. 92, Art. 1. "The Production of the Woman;" and Qu. 93, Art. 4, "The Image of God." New York: Benziger Brothers, 1947, pp. 466, 472.

[2]"Focus Form: A Study of Ministry in Communities of American Benedictine Women," Archives of the Federation of St. Scholastica. Atchison, Kansas: Mount St. Scholastica Convent,1978.

13. CONTEMPLATIVE PRAYER

In Eastern monasticism of the fourth and fifth centuries, monks most often gathered in groups around an experienced spiritual guide, an Abba or Amman, a spiritual father or mother, whose virtue had been proven and whose wisdom had become obvious for all to see. The basic form of spiritual direction among these monks of the desert was not communal but individual. The spiritual guides offered insights as they were asked by the individual monastic to facilitate growth at important junctures in the great journey to God. These "Sayings of the Desert Masters" have become spiritual classics that have withstood the tests of time.

"Father, give me a word" became the formula for growth. And those words speak to us still.

In one of the Sayings, the disciple begs the Holy One: "Master, give me a word." And the Holy One answers: "Go into your cell, and your cell will tell you all."

But, though the word is true, followers of the spiritual life know, nevertheless, that word in our day is a problem, too. If there is a temptation in the Christian life, it is probably contemplation. Physicians talk to us about "stress"; psychologists talk to us about "burnout"; sociologists talk to us about achieving "space"; educators talk to us about reflection and "process." And we all come lusting for a cave to crawl into to do it, or at least a little cottage on a hill overlooking the water, or even a small log cabin in the woods. Any place as long as it's some place appropriate; some place not here; some place simple but comfortable, of course. A place for my books, my typewriter, my tape recorder. Just me and my God. Or is it me and the gods I've made?

If there is a sin in the Christian life it is probably action. We talk about "strategizing" and "mobilizing" and "lobbying" and "renewing" and "aligning" and "reforming" as if it were all up to structures; as if action were enough. We do and do and do. And there's the problem. We set out to do something that the world needs, instead of to be something that the world needs. We set out to change instead of to illuminate. And we wonder why, with all the changes, nothing ever changes. After all the changes come, there is still the fighting, still the poverty, still the greed, still the exploitation. Why? Because deep down inside where it counts, there is still the anger, still the arrogance, still the attitudes of control. Except that now I'm the one in control. The Chinese wrote: "Now people exploit people but after the revolution it will be just the opposite."

The contemplative questions for people of action in our day are: Who will be and also do? How can we do and also be?

All we can learn by listening to ourselves in our cells is how we must grow and how we must give. The problem of this culture is that we make natural enemies out of prayer and transforming action when the two are really Siamese twins: either without the other is incomplete. But we keep trying to compartmentalize them when the purpose of life is to integrate the two.

The Desert Masters said: Seek God and not where God lives. And again they told of how a rule was once made in Scetis that the converted should fast and contemplate the entire week before Easter. During this week, however, some seekers came from Egypt to see Abba Moses and he made a modest meal for them. Seeing the smoke, the neighbors said to the priests of that place, "Look, Abba Moses has broken the rule of contemplation and is cooking food at his place." Then the priests said, "When he comes out, we will say something to him about this." And when the Sabbath came, the priests, who knew Abba Moses' great way of life, said to him in public, "Moses, you broke the commandment of contemplation made by people, but you have firmly kept the commandment to contemplate God."

Contemplation is not for its own sake. Action is no gospel of its own. Transforming action emerges from the contemplation of the gospel vision and that's why it transforms.

Transforming action is co-creative. We do not work to build up the inner city because it is a blight on the town; we work to build up the inner city because the people who live there deserve, as creatures of God, the fullness of creation. We do not serve soup in soup kitchens because the people there have qualified for free soup or because we have soup left over; we serve soup in soup kitchens because they are people and they are hungry.

Transforming action is valuable work, purposeful work, perfecting work. Things are better by the time the contemplative has finished them. Life is a little closer to the way the kingdom will look after the contemplative has been there.

Transforming action redeems the earth and all its goods: The contemplative is concerned about pollution; the contemplative cries out against militarism; the contemplative celebrates the poor; the contemplative challenges the government; the contemplative clamors for the starving. The contemplative cares and cares and cares because the gospel vision impels.

Transforming action stewards the planet and all its peoples: English and Irish, Indians and Pakistani, Vietnamese and Cambodians, Iranians and Iraqis, Libyans and Jews, Americans and Russians. Transforming action stewards the planet and all its peoples from those who would name us enemy because the gospel calls us friends.

Transforming action thirsts for justice for blacks who are unemployed, for Hispanics who are exploited, for women who are smothered in their development, for widows, for farmers, for laborers, for those born handicapped, for those born poor, for those who were never allowed to be born at all, for those born to oil the war machines of those born calloused.

Transforming action thirsts for justice because the gospel

gives voice to the voiceless. Transforming action is rooted in the mindfulness of contemplation. Transforming action comes from a whole new way of seeing. "Oh, wondrous marvel," the Zen master says, "I chop wood; I draw water from the well." The contemplative does not attempt to create a new world; the contemplative is only intent to see her own world through the eyes of God.

Contemplation without action is narcissism, pure selfishness, a religious joke. Contemplation is not time off from life; contemplation is life lived to the fullest, the deepest, from the truest of perspectives. Action without contemplation is "do-goodism," power politics, a religious charade at best. Contemplation is mindfulness of the relation between purpose and meaning. Contemplation enlarges the soul and fires the heart to lay down our lives for the gospel.

Contemplation is reaching deeply into the inner vision that gives direction to my life and bringing God to the here and now. Contemplation does not live in the there and then, in the airy, fairy nowhere. No, the function of contemplation is to bring God to the present.

Contemplation is being in the presence, and then making that presence present. Contemplation demands the response of prophetic action. To be exactly sure of what contemplation is defies possibility but it is not difficult to be sure of what contemplation is not.

Contemplation is not withdrawal, except to become more involved. Contemplation is not an emptiness that comes from "wasting time with God"; it is the fullness of awareness that comes from seeing what poverty and power and profit can do to bleach the spirit of life out of the people of God. Contemplation is not focusing on the God above; it is focusing on the God within who calls and gifts and graces us all to be gift and grace to others. Contemplation is the searing presence of the gospel in me.

There are those who ask which Jesus was the perfect model of contemplation: the Jesus in the desert or the Jesus on the mountain. There are those who ask which Jesus was the perfect model of prophetic action: the Jesus at the tomb of Lazarus or the Jesus at the cleansing of the temple. I suggest neither. Jesus the perfect model of contemplation, Jesus the perfect model of transforming action was Jesus on the cross, the Jesus who died doing the will of God for others.

And of that insight into holiness, the Desert Masters tell another parable that is word and witness for our time. The story reads:

> Past the seeker on the prayer rug, came the cripple and the beggar and the beaten. And seeing them, the Holy One went down, down, down into deep prayer and cried: "Great God! How is it that a loving Creator can see such things and yet do nothing about them?" And out of the long, long silence, God said, "I did do something about them. I made you."

Indeed, two poles of the spiritual life draw us at once. On the one hand, "Go into your cell and your cell will tell you all." And on the other, "I did do something about them. I made you." Which of these two stories we remember least as time goes on may be exactly the dimension of Christian life that we need most to develop.

14. THE WISE AND FOOLISH VIRGINS

It's been quite a period: an election has been stolen in the Philippines and our government — Chile, Vietnam, El Salvador and Haiti notwithstanding — said it would not "interfere"; budget cuts in human services are being made with hardly a blush; our "surgical strike" of Libya has killed more civilians than military; affirmative action legislation is fast being dismantled; American poor are sleeping on heating grates in the dead of winter; 27,000 American farms have disappeared with an encumbrance equal to two-thirds of the money owed by Third World countries to the United States; Russian peace proposals are being sneered into ignominy; the military budget is being increased by an administration that faults too much government and too much national debt. And what can possibly be done about it?

The papers are full of the material. Government publications themselves document the situations. The whole thing makes "Alice in Wonderland" look rational.

On the other hand, more and more people every day defy the situation. They go to jail. They withhold taxes. They challenge the laws. They go to the courts. They sit on the border of Nicaragua praying. They join Pax Christi. They reach out to one group after another trying to do something. And they get tired.

And that's where the wise and foolish virgins may be important to the peace movement.

The thing that has to be remembered about the wise and foolish virgins is that, at first, there were ten of them in the group. And they all wanted the same thing; to go to meet the bridegroom. They were of one mind. To meet the bridegroom, to be part of the bridal party, to hasten the celebration, to make the thing happen, they had to put some effort into it themselves.

They interrupted the routine of their lives. They organized. They even went together down the road.

The problem was that the foolish virgins weren't prepared to wait. They hadn't developed a spirituality for the long haul. All ten of them got tired of the deterrences along the way: the dark, the cold, the length of time the journey took. Others had the sense to make provisions for those things. But some of them did not. Some of them lacked staying power. Some of them lacked energy. Some of them lacked a fire that would not go out.

In this world of instant gratification, of pop-up tarts and microwave ovens and transatlantic flights and instant cameras, the peace movement may need to look again at the wise and foolish virgins for signs of how to travel to what is desirable but far off or slow in coming.

In the first place, we may need to be a little more feminine about the whole process. Peace above all things is not a battle we must win; it is an attitude we must build. Everyone is about peace. The generals, the Pentagon, the CIA, the companies and universities that accept military contracts — all hasten to assure the world of how badly they want peace. The question is not who wants it; the question is how we should go about getting it. And so we must be peaceful in our peacemaking.

In the second place, we must not be so serious that life's joys slip by while we are too busy to notice them. We must fish a little and sing a little and laugh quite a bit, perhaps.

We must, as well, keep as our source of energy the sight of our peaceful Christ who has gone before us to the powerful, to the politicians, to the parties, to the poor, to prayer so that the fire within us never goes out. We will not go far without oil in our own lamps, no matter how fine the company in which we travel.

We must, finally, expect it to be dark and cold and long along the way. We must be certain of where we are going and not overly depressed by failure or overly euphoric about small gains. And we must keep on: this little column, that little petition, those little conversations at the club, these little concerns about textbooks or commercials or movies or public statements.

Peacemaking is a way of life. It does not belong to those who hold membership cards; it belongs to those who watch and wait and make their own little worlds places of peace.

When will it come? The wise understand: we know neither the day nor the hour and so we must be ready.

15. THE THIRTEENTH DISCIPLE

God is not "nice."

God is not an uncle.

God is an earthquake.

If there were ever personal need of proof that the real presence of God in life brings with it the power of the earthquake, there are two scriptures that dispel all doubt.

Back to back like the pillars of the temple, like the angels at the gate, two scriptural scenes confront us with both the meaning of lay leadership and the meaning of discipleship in our lives. The first recounts the call of the disciples; the second, the cure of the demoniac in the temple. To grasp the relationship between the two, it is necessary to realize that the key to understanding the Christian call lies in the placement of the texts: You see, immediately after Jesus calls the disciples, Jesus casts out the demons. The calling of the disciples and the casting out of demons, are in actual fact, of a piece in Mark's gospel: Chapter one: Run-on lines. In other words, immediately after Jesus says: "Come follow me" he shows all of us clearly and precisely to exactly what we have been called.

And the scene is a too familiar one: In the middle of the temple, at the beginning of his ministry, right as the Son of God is starting to teach in the temple — just when and where you would not expect to find demons — the demons confront him shrieking.

Now Jesus has some choices to make: He can just ignore the

148

whole situation and pretend not to notice the intrusion; he can simply go on with the service as planned. That is what the people have come for, after all. They were "spellbound," the scriptures say. No point in losing the audience now.

Or Jesus can take another approach: He can attempt to pacify the demon. He can try to get to know it, reason with it, mollify it, set up an appointment to discuss the whole mess later when they can all "analyze" the thing "objectively." After all, this may not be either the time or the place to upset the church. Issues like this have divided churches in the past, you know.

Or finally, Jesus can choose to bring truth to power: he can face the demon down; he can expel it then and there.

Jesus says, "Come out of that man!" And there on the spot, in the midst of the disciples, in the midst of the temple, in the midst of the people the demon is defeated. Jesus chooses to dare discipleship rather than to traffic in a false sense of church. Faced with a demon, Jesus refuses to consort with the evil in front of him. Jesus refuses to call it acceptable or even uncertain, doubtful, and unclear for any other number of gains: not for political approval, not for social acceptance, not for public face. Jesus simply refuses to accept the sick in this society and by doing nothing about it to name it health. Jesus says there is no discipleship worth having that settles for unsettling truths.

And then an interesting thing happens: the demon blames Jesus for causing the trouble: "What are you trying to do to us, Jesus of Nazareth? Have you come to destroy us?" And in those brief verses lie the paradigm of Christian leadership and the call to discipleship that is with us yet today.

Christian leadership and gospel discipleship have little or nothing to do with the collection of theological footnotes and the composition of church creeds. Christian leadership is much more meaningful than that. Christian leadership has something to do with our coming together as disciples of the gospel of Christ — with different charisms, of course; with distinct qualities, certainly; from different Christian communities, yes! But coming together and together casting out the demons of our time.

Discipleship depends on our settling for nothing less than the gospel of Jesus Christ despite those who look to the church for its good news but resist its full demands. And, oh, oftener than not, Christian discipleship depends on our realizing that when we finally recognize the demon and set out to cast it out, that, like Jesus, in all likelihood the trouble will be blamed on us.

> Do you stand for nuclear disarmament?
> — What are you trying to do:
> — Destroy the country?

> Do you stand for the rights of women?
> — What are you trying to do:
> — Destroy the family?

> Do you stand for the just distribution of resources?
> — What are you trying to do:
> — Destroy the "American way?"

> Do you stand for civil rights?
> — What are you trying to do:
> — Destroy the cities?

What are you trying to do to us, Jesus of Nazareth? Are you trying to destroy us?

For the unity it took to cast out the demons of the day, Jesus called twelve disciples together. But, scripture reminds us always of the need for the thirteenth.

Today, it is Martin Luther King who shows us still what the thirteenth disciple is like.

The thirteenth disciple walks the streets with the hungry, and because of that leadership the whole church walks there, too. The thirteenth disciple cries to heaven for the wounded, and because of that discipleship, full and empowered, the whole church can cry out, too. The thirteenth disciple storms the very capitol of this country if need be, if no one will listen, if no one will stop the injustice, the inequity, and the inhumanities it takes to keep the poor, poor and the weak, weak. But, most of all, perhaps, the thirteenth disciple — like Jesus — makes of all of us rag-tag followers, us basically satisfied, essentially concerned but highly individualistic temple-goers a community of prophets. No, a prophetic community. A people of God whose differences welded together in Christ become a light to the nations, a new Jerusalem, a chosen race.

To be disciple it is not enough to do theology; it is not enough to do church; it is not enough to do good. To be disciples we must do the gospel together.

In an era where Christians are less than one-third of the world population, the question is not: Will we be a sign? The only question is: What kind of sign will Christianity be? Will the sign of the Christian church at the turn of the century be a collection of the individually pious, as good as that is? Will our sign to a poor and starving world be a cadre of Christian chauvinists claiming only for themselves the full revelation of God as provincially empowering, pre-occupying, potent, and pre-possessing as that is? Or will the Christian sign to the twenty-first century be the church united together in Christ — its people, its priests, its religious — for the coming of the kingdom; for the present reign of God; for the casting out of demons? Now.

Do we want church unity? Then we must look to this day's thirteenth disciple. Martin Luther King made one church out of the many churches for the casting out of demons. Martin Luther King didn't sit around talking about Eucharist making us a community; Martin Luther King showed us that community makes us Eucharist. Martin Luther King didn't talk about unity. Martin Luther King unified a country divided and did it the hard way — by gathering Christians together to cast out its demons.

He protested a war waged by the armed against the defense-
less. And in that the churches found the gospel. He cried out
loud for the poor too hungry and too cold and too sick and too
invisible to cry for themselves. And in that the church found its
gospel. He walked and worked and wrung out his soul for
human rights in this world, in our world. And in that the church
found its gospel. And so Martin Luther King showed us what
Christian leadership is. Martin Luther King unified us; Martin
Luther King made disciples of us all.

Is it the Gospel we want? Is it discipleship we want? Then let
us — you and me — be about the casting out of demons together.
Where most of the poor are Black, how can we say that racism is
not still our demon? Where most of the powerless are women,
how can we say that sexism is not our demon? Where most of the
resources of this nation — human, financial, and physical — go
to destruction instead of to development, how can we say that
militarism is not our demon?

Let us in our day cast out from our temples the demon of
planned planetary destruction that is masked in our midst as
"defense" and "deterrence." There is no defense in deterrence
and no deterrence in a defense that destroys our culture and our
capacity for cooperation and our souls as it goes.

Let us in our day cast out from our world the demon of poverty
of soul that is masked in our lives as corporate profit making and
so takes resources and takes lives and takes the future from the
poor.

Let us in our day cast out from our lives the demon of exploitation that is masked in our hearts as male and female "roles" so
that some of us are treated as more human than the rest of us.

Let us in our day cast out from our country and our churches
and our hearts the demons of militarism and racism and sexism
that separate and divide and shrink us all, while scholars collect
footnotes and privatized religion has a spree.

The only thing lacking in church leadership today is once

again a thirteenth disciple who will gather the different disciples for the casting out of demons together.

But with Martin dead and Ghandi gone and Samantha Smith ungrown, who of us can possibly be ready for leadership like that? The days of great dreamers, great doers, are perhaps done. And if so, then what of Christian leadership and what of discipleship now?

Well, I don't know. The list of those ready to make people into a prophetic church has always been short. It is good to remember as we struggle with the false humility of powerlessness, that not even Jesus found "the ready."

Jesus called Nathaniel, the recliner,
   the prejudiced one.
"Can anything good come out of Nazareth?"
   Nathaniel said.
Nathaniel lacked openness. Nathaniel wasn't ready.

Jesus called Philip, the patriot.
Philip wanted Jesus to be king, not the Nazarene.
Philip lacked simplicity. Philip wasn't ready.

Jesus called Simon, the Zealot.
Simon thought redemption required military and
   political force.
Simon lacked non-violence. Simon wasn't ready.

Jesus called Andrew, the cynic.
"Five loaves and two fishes! What can anyone do with
   that?" Andrew said.
Andrew lacked a sense of risk. Andrew wasn't ready.

Jesus called Thomas, the doubter.
Thomas couldn't see beyond the obvious.
Thomas lacked vision. Thomas wasn't ready.

Jesus called Judas, the pragmatist.
Judas didn't want God; Judas wanted good business

practices: "This perfume could have been sold
for 300 denarii."
Judas lacked spiritual maturity.
Judas was definitely not ready.

Jesus called Matthew, the tax collector.
Matthew had spent his whole life succeeding
    at the expense of others.
Matthew lacked a sense of social sin.
Matthew wasn't ready.

Jesus called Thaddeus, the realist.
Thaddeus was looking for credibility and certification
    but definitely not prophecy.
Thaddeus asks: "Why don't you reveal yourself to the
world?"
— a loose translation of which is: "You tell them who
    you are. Don't leave the burden to us!"
Thaddeus lacked commitment.
Thaddeus wasn't ready.

Jesus called James the Lesser, the chauvinist.
James insisted that Christianity was only for the
    Jews.
James had no notion whatsoever of world redemp-
    tion.
James lacked awareness. James wasn't ready.

Jesus called James and John, the sons of thunder.
James and John were well on their way to becoming
    career ministers, ambitious men who wanted
    a good church position.
James and John were buckin' to be bishop.
James and John lacked a sense of servanthood.
James and John were not ready.

Jesus called Peter, the Rock.
And Peter? Peter wanted to lead the leader on his
    own terms.

"Don't go up to Jerusalem, Jesus," Peter said.
Peter lacked courage. Peter was not ready.

And in our time, Jesus called Martin Luther King,
   the dreamer.
But Martin suffered bout after bout of depression,
because Martin often lacked hope in the face of
   defeat.
Martin Luther King was not ready.

The point, you see, is that Jesus doesn't call the ready. Jesus
calls the willing. Jesus didn't call the individuals as individuals.
Jesus took the disciples in their individual weaknesses and
made out of them a powerful — no, an empowering — church.
And if Christianity is to be Christianity we, you and I, your
church and mine, must do the same. Do we really want Christian leadership? Do we really want discipleship? Then the world
is waiting to see you here and I there each in our own local
church stand up, with all the others, for the Gospel questions of
our time.

Do Christians really want peace? Then when will we stand for
it as churches together? For all the world and our own government to see?

Do Christians want justice for the poor and deprived? Then
when will we lead by joining hands across the scriptures of Amos
and Micah and Isaiah to get it?

Do Christians want a world of friends or a world of enemies; a
world of the living or a world of the dead? Then let the Christian
church, the Pentecost Church let its differences shine together
in the name of Christ.

Jesus taught with authority, read the scriptures, and the
people listened. When will we all together take the authority of
those same teachings to a world preparing to arm the heavens;
to a world substituting weapons for wheat; to a world that en-
slaves the poor for the profit of the powerful; to a world where

half its people, women, have little or nothing to do with the political and military decisions which will destroy them — and all in the name of God.

When will our churches bring the Gospel to our time? If the people will lead, eventually the leaders will follow.

Do we really want discipleship? Do we really want Christian leadership? Then it is for you and for me, for Congregationalists and Catholics and Methodists and Presbyterians and Episcopalians and Lutherans together now that the world waits to see the credibility, the conscience, the Christ of Christianity.

It is you and I as leaders and disciples together that the demons fear.

God is not "nice."

God is not an uncle.

God is an earthquake.